LOOKING AT LONERGAN'S METHOD

LOOKING AT LONERGAN'S METHOD

Edited by
PATRICK CORCORAN S.M.

Wipf & Stock
PUBLISHERS
Eugene, Oregon

Wipf and Stock Publishers
199 W 8th Ave, Suite 3
Eugene, OR 97401

Looking at Lonergan's Method
By Corcoran, Patrick, SM
Copyright©1975 Educational Company of Ireland
ISBN 13: 978-1-55635-319-2
ISBN 10: 1-55635-319-1
Publication date 3/6/2007
Previously published by Talbot Press, 1975

Contents

PART ONE: INTRODUCTORY

Foreword   7
Patrick Corcoran, S.M.

Chapter 1   *Method in Theology* in the Lonergan *corpus*   11
David F. Ford

PART TWO: PHILOSOPHICAL CONSIDERATIONS

Chapter 2   Knowledge, understanding and reality: some questions concerning Lonergan's philosophy   27
Patrick McGrath

Chapter 3   Lonergan's notion of being in relation to his method   42
N. D. O'Donoghue, O.D.C.

Chapter 4   A note on Lonergan and a Greek conception of science   55
Gerard Watson

PART THREE: METHODOLOGICAL CONSIDERATIONS

Chapter 5   Lonergan and method in the natural sciences   59
Mary Hesse

Chapter 6   Theological disagreement and the functional specialities   73
Elizabeth Maclaren

Chapter 7   History and meaning in Bernard Lonergan's approach to theological method   88
Wolfhart Pannenberg

Chapter 8   The function of inner and outer word in Lonergan's theological method   101
T. F. Torrance

PART FOUR: THEOLOGICAL CONSIDERATIONS

Chapter 9   Method and cultural discontinuity   127
            N. Lash

Chapter 10 Divine revelation and Lonergan's transcendental
            method in theology   144
            J. P. Mackey

Chapter 11 Some questions on the place of believing
            experience in the work of Bernard Lonergan   164
            J. P. Jossua, O.P.

Chapter 12 'Conversion'   175
            Donal Dorr, S.S.P.

Chapter 13 Front-line theology: a marginal comment on
            Newman and Lonergan   187
            John Coulson

Foreword

Patrick Corcoran, SM.

Bernard Lonergan is a name which is being dropped increasingly in theological circles. Theology has its Hall of Fame: entry to it comes when a man having written about theology becomes himself an object of research. In this hall there are many mansions. Some have their assured niches there; their achievement and their importance have stood the test of time, indeed of centuries. The portraits of others may stand in the foyer for a time, only to be relegated for all time to gather dust in the basement.

Bernard Lonergan is a theologian of our time, and estimates of the depth and durability of his achievement vary. This collection of essays is one effort to assess that achievement. It hopes to expose Lonergan's thought to a wide variety of traditions. Lonergan is a Canadian Jesuit and the works which mark his special contribution to theology are written in English. The fact that he is a Catholic theologian writing in English has, for some years now, tended to restrict his impact. It has been said that there is no common market in philosophy, and this has also been true in large measure of theology. More accurately such trade as existed in theology was largely oneway — with continental writers operating in a seller's market. For some years now Catholic theology in English has been experiencing the kind of situation that Herbert Butterfield has described:

> It was often noted in the earlier decades of the present century how greatly it had become the habit of Protestants to hold some German scholar up their sleeves — a different one every few years but always preferably the latest one — and at appropriate moments strike the unwary philistine on the head with their secret weapon, the German scholar having decided in a final manner whatever point might have been at issue in a controversy. From all of which the charge arose that for Protestants the unanswerable pope was always some professor — a system more inconvenient than that of Rome, partly because the seat of authority might change overnight, and be transferred to a new teacher who had never been heard of before, and partly, if one has to have a pope, it is at least

better that he should be subject to certain rules and traditions and appointed by a properly constituted authority.[1]

For some time now Catholic theology in English conveys the impression that theological agility consists in picking up kites that German scholars have abandoned or are on the point of abandoning. More recently there have been signs of some reversal of this trend. One such sign is the increasing degree in which continental writers are recycling material headlined in English-speaking theology in recent years: one thinks of the aftermath of *Honest to God*, the Death of God theology, and process theology. There is an incipient interest too on the continent in Bernard Lonergan. This is, in part, an echo of the debate that has been going on in English-speaking Catholic circles, and in part due to the area that Lonergan has cultivated, which poses questions about the foundations of theology.

Among English-speaking Catholics themselves Bernard Lonergan is a sign of contradiction: there is cult and anti-cult, and he is sometimes used against the 'unwary philistine'. The Lonergan *corpus* consists of various works in Latin, and others in English such as *Insight* and *Method in Theology*. While the Latin works bear the individual impress of Lonergan it is to the works in English that one looks for the more specific contribution he makes to theology. The very titles suggest a difficult area, and there is little in the debate about Lonergan that makes it any less difficult.

The present book has grown out of a Seminar held at St. Patrick's College, Maynooth, Ireland, in the Spring of 1973. This Seminar, which owes so much to the initiative and the energy of Paul Surlis, exposed Lonergan's thought and more specifically the contribution of his *Method in Theology* to the assessment of scholars from differing traditions and disciplines. It brought together theologians, continental and English-speaking, Catholics and Protestants, philosophers and scientists. The essays in this volume were not delivered to the Seminar: they represent the writers' reflections in the light of the exchanges at the Seminar, and their study of Lonergan's *Method in Theology*. The division of labour suggests itself readily, if we keep in mind that it is not possible to make hermetically sealed departments: certain constants run right through Lonergan's thought and some overlap is inevitable.

The preliminary essay by David F. Ford reminds us of the

Lonergan 'context': one cannot read his works in isolation. They belong to a *corpus* and while there is progress there is also continuity, in which the later works presuppose positions staked out in the earlier ones.

Ford also insists with justice that 'If Lonergan's philosophy is seriously mistaken the method collapses.' Lonergan belongs to the group loosely designated as transcendental Thomists, who endeavour to combine the insights of Kant and St. Thomas. There are those like Etienne Gilson who think that this is an unstable mixture: there is, he maintains, no half-way house between St. Thomas and Kant. Our contributors do not address this question: their interest is directed to determining whether Lonergan's philosophy offers stable or shaky foundations on which to build. P. J. McGrath's essay studies the ambiguities in Lonergan concerning knowledge, understanding and reality. Noel Dermot O'Donoghue O.D.C., considers his metaphysics, and Gerard Watson examines a possible confusion in Lonergan's use of the term science in the Greek context.

A book such as *Method in Theology* calls for an investigation of the validity of Lonergan's methodology. One aspect of his work that has impressed many theologians is the ease with which he seems to move in mathematical and scientific circles. Mary Hesse makes a critical assessment of this side of his work. Elizabeth Maclaren has reservations about the capacity of Lonergan's method to account sufficiently for theological disagreement. Wolfhart Pannenberg asks whether Lonergan has seen meaning and method in a horizon that is comprehensive enough to offer an acceptable method in theology. T. F. Torrance follows Lonergan's attempt to find a third way for theology between the classical concept of science and empirical science.

It is sometimes said that Lonergan's method is radical but his theology is conservative. In the debate about Lonergan, even more than in Lonergan's own writings, there is the vague sensation of a theological drag hunt in which there is a certain amount of scent but no quarry. It is said that theology disappears under technology. People ask: what difference does Lonergan's method make to theology, how would theology look if Lonergan's method is followed?

Another attitude — and it corresponds to the preoccupations of N. Lash and J. P. Mackey — is that however radical Lonergan may seem he is not radical enough to give us a theology that is viable today. B. Dorr and J. P. Jossua from different angles examine one of Lonergan's basic categories, 'conversion'. Finally, John Coulson opens an interesting avenue with his article which underlines points of contact between Newman and Lonergan.

Some of these contributions have already appeared in the *Irish Theological Quarterly*. My best thanks are due to P. McGoldrick, the editor, for permission to reprint them here, and also for his sterling work, at all stages of the enterprise, which made my task considerably easier.

NOTE

1 *Christianity and History* 1964=1949, p. 19.

Method in Theology in the Lonergan Corpus

David F. Ford

I

The main aim of this contribution is to clarify some of what *Method in Theology* has to say about the related topics of grace, conversion and the existence of God by referring to Lonergan's earlier works. I will also point to some of the ecumenical implications of Lonergan's latest positions on these topics.

Lonergan has written a good deal more than has been published, and some of his publications, especially those in Latin, have had a very limited circulation.[1] Fortunately, there is now a Lonergan Centre in Regis College, Toronto, where there are collected all Lonergan's work and tape recordings of some of his lectures, together with his private papers, notes and sermons over the past forty years.[2] There is material there for an intellectual biography which would help in appreciating his publications, especially in avoiding misunderstanding of his development. One of the most interesting facts to emerge is the depth of his concern all through his career for pressing modern problems, such as those of economics. For instance, underlying the remarks on economics in Ch. VII of *Insight* is a 152-page original study of the circulation of goods.

However, in examining *Method in Theology* in the Lonergan corpus, there are in my opinion only two indispensable works, *Grace and Freedom*[3] and *Insight*.[4] The Latin works on Christology and the Trinity[5] show what Lonergan has produced by applying his own precepts, though always with the reservation that they were written before February, 1965, when his thought on theological method crystallized into its present form. His remaining major work, *Verbum*,[6] is largely, as far as relevance to *Method in Theology* is concerned, taken up into *Insight*. On the subject of how these works fit into the whole *corpus* there is a comprehensive book by David Tracy[7] which is all the more useful because Tracy wrote it with the knowledge of most of what was to be in *Method*, and interprets Lonergan's works from a theological viewpoint as leading up to his latest work. This article will keep to the topics of the first paragraph and assume that those who want an overall view of Lonergan's achievement will read Tracy.

THE PLACE OF CONVERSION

The importance of *Grace and Freedom* for *Method* is in giving content to the controversial theological principle of conversion. In two key passages[8] on conversion Lonergan refers the reader to *Grace and Freedom*. He therefore explicitly carries over the context of Aquinas doctrine of grace into *Method*. Lonergan is here making clear a major element in his own understanding of conversion, and is pointing to where the debate must be continued: over his interpretation of and agreement with Aquinas. So far this debate has not taken place — indeed there has been no systematic study of Lonergan's theology. Yet even supposing that one disagrees with *Grace and Freedom* on the relation of nature to grace one might still adopt the theological method. This is so because to have a theological principle at all, something must be said about it, but, in his response to the first volume of Florida papers Lonergan is clear that he does not intend his Thomist understanding to influence the results obtained by using the method:

> It is not the methodologist's views on religious conversion, any more than those of Aquinas or Luther or Calvin or some introspective psychologist, but conversion itself and its spontaneous consequences that exerts an influence on the results of research, interpretation, history and dialectic.[9]

The effect of this is to push the event of conversion outside any functional specialty. Lonergan's own earlier drafts of the structure of *Method* show that he first of all had Conversion as the fourth specialty, but later rejected this.[10] Now its place is in Ch. IV on religion, though, of course, it is of the greatest importance for Dialectics and Foundations. It is something simply given by God which cannot be critically justified except by the subject of the experience: 'The gift itself is self-justifying.'[11] In this way it is parallel to the self-affirmation of Ch. XI of *Insight*[12] — either it happens or its does not, and if not, then Lonergan says that the essential condition for assessing his work has not been fulfilled.

The placing of the event of conversion outside the operation of any specialty makes all formulations of it radically open to debate, and so ensures the theological neutrality of Dialectics and Foundations. Lonergan's own formulation of a distinction between faith, which springs from the love of God given in religious conversion, and beliefs which are judgments of value that come from faith, is, however, far from neutral, and is one place where he goes beyond Aquinas. A key passage for comparison with *Method* is the section on conversion in *Grace and Freedom*.[13] This says that in the process of conversion, 'the first act does not presuppose any object apprehended by the intellect; God acts directly on the radical orientation of the will.'[14] This position is not that of the 'major exception' to *nihil amatum nisi praecognitum*,[15] because the 'first act' is *Dei operatio convertentis cor*, and the *motus charitatis* does not come till after the intellect's *motus fidei*.[16] Thus, Lonergan's present position of 'another kind of knowledge'[17] being given by the gift of God's love might seem to reverse the order of faith and love, giving love a new cognitive status. This makes possible the distinction between faith ('the knowledge born of religious love'[18]) and beliefs. The distinction is already a centre of debate. For instance, Bishop Butler makes it his chief criticism of *Method*, due to a fear for the centrality of Christian revelation,[19] a fear which is also present in Karl Rahner's comments on the functional specialties.[20] George Vass sees the distinction as the proof that 'Lonergan has thrown in his lot with Schleiermacher and with the liberal tradition in theology which followed in his wake'.[21] So it is worthwhile trying to find out what content Lonergan gives to the distinction.

The issue turns out to be the crucial test case of Lonergan's thought as distilled in *Grace and Freedom*, *Insight* and *Method*. For what he seems to say is: I am retaining the content of *Grace and Freedom*, transposing it into the horizon of interiority that *Insight* was written to facilitate, and finally bringing interiority to the limits of the subject-centred stance represented by *Method*.[22] The point of departure in *Grace and Freedom* for the later developments is the fact that the first act of conversion is *Dei operatio convertentis cor*. In later terminology this means conscious entry into a new horizon, and this experience is put first as the ground of faith and of the acceptance of all subsequent beliefs. Lonergan's new position does not, however, put all this weight on such an interpretation of the first act. Rather he invokes his interpretation of western intellectual history up to the time when 'intentionality analysis routed faculty psychology',[23] and puts Aquinas' account of conversion into a new context. Aquinas analysed conversion metaphysically in terms of faculty psychology, in which were raised such questions as the precedence of intellect over will, to be answered by the precedence of the *motus fidei* over the *motus charitatis*. In a technical note[24] Lonergan briefly explains the translation of Aquinas into the four levels of intentional consciousness whose relationships are fixed without questions of initiative or precedence being settled. 'Significant change on any level calls for adjustments on other levels, and the order in which the adjustments take place depends mostly on the readiness with which they can be effected.'[25] Yet because the fourth level sublates the other three and is responsible for their proper functioning[26] it is the key to conversion. The new form of analysis permits a new order of precedence appealing to the exceptional experience of conversion in which love precedes knowledge.

> Because we acknowledge interiority as a distinct realm of meaning, we can begin with a description of religious experience, acknowledge a dynamic state of being in love without restrictions, and later identify this state with the state of sanctifying grace.[27]

LONERGAN AND SCHLEIERMACHER

Schleiermacher, too, began with a description of religious experience, and it is no accident that his name should be raised in discussing Lonergan. Schleiermacher was the first theologian to face up to the post-Kantian era of critical philosophy which Lonergan sees as a shift to interiority. Many of Schleiermacher's critics, such as Karl Barth, see Christianity's distinctiveness and transcendence threatened by a theology beginning from human consciousness. Has Lonergan made Christianity one among many religions, all of them with different ways of formulating the same subjective state? Vass interprets him thus: 'Grace, without being explicitly *gratia Christi*, is a human possibility. It preempts conversion to Jesus Christ, and considered as love it has no personal focus but the human self who feels himself to be in love.'[28]

There is some irony in Lonergan, a Jesuit professor of dogmatic theology with rather conservative views, being accused of capitulating to liberal Protestantism. Lonergan himself, replying to Langdon Gilkey's suggestion that he is returning to Schleiermacher's ideas, saw the main difference as philosophical; Schleiermacher's

Kantian concept of knowledge does not permit genuine transcendence, but *Insight* tries to show how this can be overcome.[29] On the charge of subjectivism, Lonergan's whole philosophy can be seen as an attempt to show that objectivity in every field of knowledge is the result of authentic subjectivity, and in *Method* he sums this up by saying: 'To attempt to ensure objectivity apart from self-transcendence only generates illusions.'[30]

However, Lonergan's description of religious conversion, as the work of grace inverting the normal cognitional process by beginning with falling in love, keeps the issue open. For the change from faculty psychology to intentionality analysis is not the only advance in *Grace and Freedom*: there is also the fact that in *Grace and Freedom* the grace is explicitly Christian, but in *Method* it is grace that works conversion in other religions too. To be a Christian one needs the further transformation of conversion to Christ, but non-Christians can certainly be saved. Lonergan's expression of universalist faith is of course just one approach to a long-standing issue within theology, on which Schleiermacher also had much to say. But it is very important that Lonergan's conclusions on it are not seen as integral to the theological method. A theologian who recognizes only Christian conversion as genuine is not ruled out methodologically, and for him the distinction between faith and beliefs might even still be valid in ecumenism. Likewise Bishop Butler's views on the sacramental nature of conversion do not contradict the method's principles although they give a narrower interpretation than Lonergan's.[31] The issue that is integral is the transcendence of God. Can this be maintained within a subject-centred method? As I said above, Lonergan's answer is that in *Insight* he shows how it can be done. Charles Curran,[32] however, has complained that Lonergan uses two conflicting terminologies about conversion, one of progress and development, the other of discontinuity and complete re-direction. This paradox in the face of the relationship of nature to grace is also Thomist, but as if in anticipation of the accusation (frequent against Schleiermacher) of making divine operation into an anthropological principle, Lonergan has in *Method* put far more emphasis on the discontinuity between the two than he did in *Insight*. There are fifty-nine references under 'gift' in the index of *Method*. This is Lonergan's way of denying anthropological reductionism. The new emphasis has the effect of revising *Insight* in a way that will appear later. Lonergan's meaning is, however, plain throughout his works. He always adheres strictly to the 'theorem of transcendence'. Much of his effort has gone into trying to handle intelligently two problems which remain mysteries, that of the transcendence of God, which has an excess of intelligibility, and that of evil which lacks intelligibility.[33] So it is necessary to give to the new terminology of *Method* the content which can be supplied from his other works,[34] and in any conflict between the apparent implication of *Method's* approach and his earlier positions it is safest to assume that his meaning has not changed. On transcendence and subjectivism his intentions are clear, but whether his philosophy works or not is a matter for personal verification. The major battle over whether his subject-centred philosophy and theological method can do justice to Christian revelation must be fought over *Insight,* for only then can one begin to assess the claim that the method is theologically neutral.

This alleged neutrality is the source of the radical criticism of the method expressed by Rahner.[35] Where does Christ come in? It seems intolerable not to make Christ explicitly central. Lonergan's view is that Christ will be central if the theologian has undergone Christian, moral and intellectual conversion, and that no other foundation than this can ensure Christ's place in theology.[36] Here again we come up against two facts: that the event of conversion is outside the method's set of operations and yet of the greatest importance for them, and that the philosophical basis given in *Insight* must be accepted if the method is to make sense.

Two conclusions result from this section. First, by making religious and Christian conversion fundamental, and yet also both completely dependent on God's grace and not among the operations of any specialty, Lonergan has kept all formulation of conversion (including his own transposed Thomism with its corollary of the distinction between faith and beliefs) radically open to debate without the validity of the method itself being called in question. Secondly, however, there are two conditions which must be fulfilled before conversion can be granted this position: the occurrence of religious and Christian conversion, and agreement with Lonergan's philosophy, or intellectual conversion. To the critic who does not assent to at least the first thirteen chapters of *Insight* Lonergan will seem to commit grave theological errors in the name of the shift to interiority. The Schleiermacher issue raised by Gilkey and

Vass is an example of how Lonergan sees as a philosophical position what for his critics is a fundamental theological option. The problem of Christ's place in a Christian theological method is similar. The next section will show that *Insight* should be read differently in the light of *Method*, but this will not mean that Lonergan has lowered the level of required philosophical agreement. On the contrary, authentic use of the transcendental method described in Ch. I of *Method* demands 'a struggle with some such book as *Insight*',[37] and all the subsequent chapters of *Method* are 'prolongations of the first'.[38] This demand is always likely to remain the chief stumbling-block to acceptance of the method.

FROM *INSIGHT* TO *METHOD*

If Lonergan's philosophy is seriously mistaken, the method collapses. It is clear, too, that his philosophy is by no means theologically neutral. The clearest example of this is the culmination of *Insight* in Chaps. XIX and XX which are claimed to show 'the inevitability with which the affirmation of God and the search of intellect for faith arise out of a sincere acceptance of scientific presuppositions and precepts'.[39] However, the new emphasis on religious conversion has not left this philosophy unaffected, and the whole subject of natural theology has been put into a new context. *Method* gives the end product of a long process: now conversion, not proof, is basic, and there is to be 'an integration of natural with systematic theology'. There is still a distinction between the two,[40] but the critical point is that both are done after conversion. 'Proof becomes rigorous only within a systematically formulated horizon', and the converted horizon 'is never the logical consequence of one's previous position but, on the contrary, a radical revision of that position'.[41] So from the point of view of horizons analysis it is much better to see Lonergan's theology implying a philosophy rather than *vice versa*. All his philosophizing has been as a Christian, he sees his philosophical attitude implied by Christianity,[42] and major influences on his early philosophical thought were Augustine, Aquinas, and Newman.

In this perspective, *Method's* new position with natural theology as a part of systematics is just making explicit what was Lonergan's tendency all along. Yet Charles Davis was perceptive about Lonergan's cognitional structure when he said that 'a revision may be "incidental" in relation to the basic abstract scheme, but of the weightiest consequence in relation to actual human knowing'.[43] Such an apparently incidental change has, I think, occurred in *Method's* emphasis on conversion and the level of decision and responsibility. One of the chief criticisms of John Wren-Lewis in his early review of *Insight* was that it did not admit that 'true objectivity comes through direct *emotional* encounter with what is other than ourselves'.[44] That is now provided by the gift of God's love bringing another kind of knowledge which is self-justifying. It still fits within the scheme of *Insight,* but brings great changes with it. I will deal with two areas of change, on the existence of God and ecumenism. In an interview in 1970 Lonergan said: 'I think Ch. XIX was mainly the product of an entirely different type of thinking. I'd be quite ready to say: Let's drop Ch. XIX out of *Insight* and put it inside of theology.'[45] In *Method* that is what he has done, but without explicitly correcting *Insight*. So it is worthwhile, for the sake of those who take Lonergan's advice, to prepare for *Method* by struggling through *Insight,* to explain why Ch. XIX does not measure up to the claims made for it in *Insight*.

The reason is that the affirmation of the existence of God should be 'virtually unconditioned', but actually does not allude to the condition which from the reader's point of view is most important of all, that he already be religiously converted. That is the only horizon within which the proof can be rigorous. In other words, *Insight* is not sufficiently subject-centred. The book is designed as an experiment to be performed by the reader, who is not asked to accept anything he has not verified for himself. The principle throughout is that the fact proves the possibility.[46] For Lonergan, as a Christian, the possibility of affirming God's existence was a fact from the first sentence of the book, and he could, from within that horizon, see that with the two steps of self-affirmation, and the identification of the real and the intelligible with being, 'knowledge of God's existence makes its implicit entry'.[47] But how is this implication made explicit for the reader? Only by progress through a succession of higher viewpoints. In Ch. XVIII 'the empirically, intelligently, rationally conscious subject of self-affirmation becomes a morally self-conscious subject'.[48] The next chapter then ignores the implied existential condition if the reader is to affirm with certainty God as, among other things, the 'lovable good'[49] who demands to be loved. That chapter is therefore not a higher viewpoint but what Tracy calls 'a quite distinct enterprise — namely, a reformulation of the traditional Thomist argument for the existence of God in the context of Lonergan's reformulated notion of causality and the philosophical implications of the "position" on intellectual conversion'.[50]

It is important to note why in Lonergan's philosophy this distinct enterprise is so unsatisfactory. It is because his system cannot be content with proving a possibility. The ultimate argument against the existence of God is that the universe is just a brute fact. Lonergan's version of a brute fact is an inverse insight,[51] and it is a possibility that an inverse insight might be the answer to the question of God's existence.[52] The only convincing answer that Lonergan can give to this is that this possibility can be forgotten because in fact we can affirm God's existence: 'The proof of the possibility lies in the fact that such intelligent grasp and reasonable affirmation occur.'[53]

This event did not occur in Lonergan before his religious conversion, and he regards this as normal, though in order to accommodate Vatican I he makes an exception and reverts to talking in terms of possibility:

> I should say that normally religious conversion precedes the effort to work out rigorous proofs for the existence of God. But I do not think it impossible that such proofs might be a factor facilitating religious conversion so that, by way of exception, certain knowledge of God's existence should precede the acceptance of God's gift of his love.[54]

The uncharacteristically hesitant tone of this statement contrasts with *Insight's* confident march to prove God's existence. In *Method* the focus is on God's gift of his love. Transcendence is still 'the elementary matter of raising further questions',[55] but we have 'the question of God in a new form', that of the call to decide whether or not to respond to him, and 'only secondarily do there arise the questions of God's existence and nature'.[56] This completes the transition from *Insight,* and critics are left facing a new synthesis of philosophy and theology which is compared to that of Aquinas,[57] but which has a new foundation explicitly demanding radical self-involvement. Only occasionally, as on Vatican I, is there a retreat from the subject-centred approach to step outside and have a look at what might be possible but is not verifiable. Proof and rigorous argument have not been denied, and philosophy is not swallowed up by theology, but there is a change in the fulcrum of Lonergan's thought. Now conversions of different types are central, and it is not surprising that one of the big questions is about the theological implications (e.g. in the direction of Schleiermacher) of this Christian philosophy.

To sum up this section, what is the novelty of *Method* as compared with *Insight*? It is that now the Christian context of Lonergan's philosophy is shown by the marriage of systematic and natural theology, and the implications of the subject-centred stance are followed to the limit of making conversions foundational for theology. These changes have the seeds of developments that would never have seemed possible if *Insight* had been Lonergan's final word. The next section deals with one such case.

ECUMENISM

I will now try to bring together the strands of this article as they combine in the theme of ecumenism. Bishop Butler wrote of *Insight*: 'It is, however, sufficiently obvious that anyone who has followed and accepted his argumentation will, at the end of it, face an obligation — if he is not already a Catholic — to make contact with a Catholic priest and seek admission to the Church.'[58] This would seem to be Lonergan's hope of *Insight* too, because the last chapter builds up inexorably to this conclusion. *Method*, however, sees neither Ch. XIX's proof of the existence of God nor, *a fortiori*, Ch. XX's arrival at Rome, as so straightforward a matter. Both chapters are transposed to Systematics, and so are preceded by six specialties, with Dialectics being especially relevant to ecumenism.

The interest in ecumenism is a new note in Lonergan's work. It is inherent in the very conception of the 'methodical exigence'. A theology fixated at the systematic stage[59] will not be open to the sort of understanding of itself and of opposed theologies that the chapter on Dialectics demands. The lack of interest of many conservative theologians in ecumenism is an example of this. A theology fixated at the critical stage is hardly likely to be concerned with reconciling large systems of thought and doctrine. The lack of interest of many radical theologians in the doctrinal issues dividing churches is an example of this. However, the methodical approach proposed by Lonergan demands that facing up to past and present conflicts among Christians be the culmination of the activities of researchers, interpreters and historians.

Lonergan says in his Introduction: 'The method I indicate is, I think, relevant to more than Roman Catholic theologians.' [60] Elsewhere in the book further ecumenical claims are made: that 'by distinguishing faith and belief we have secured a basis for ecumenical encounter' [61]; that 'the basis of Christian ecumenism' is found in the joining of 'the inner gift of God's love with its outer manifestation in Christ Jesus and in those who follow him' [62]; and the book ends with an optimistic section on ecumenism.

All this does not indicate a new ecumenical phase in Lonergan's own theology, which has from the first been preoccupied in a remarkably single-minded way with his own tradition. He has approached the problem of the confrontation of Christianity and modern man mainly through philosophy and the sciences, on the one hand, and the achievement of Aquinas on the other hand. There has been remarkably little dialogue with the Protestant thinkers who have been facing the same questions posed by post-classical civilization. In *Method* he gives several summary verdicts on Protestant theologians, the most significant of which is that Barth and Bultmann, while they 'both acknowledged the significance of moral and religious conversion' yet lack intellectual conversion: 'Only intellectual conversion can remedy Barth's fideism. Only intellectual conversion can remove the secularist notion of scientific exegesis represented by Bultmann.' [63] Here again *Insight* is revealed as the rock upon which *Method* is built, but it is also worthwhile noting the effects of the novelties of *Method*. The way in which natural theology is treated means, for instance, that Barth is not disqualified from the start. One of the most profound ecumenical discussions of Barth, that by Hans Urs von Balthasar,[64] deals at length with Barth's characterization of Roman Catholic theology as inauthentic because of its dependence on the *analogia entis,* and traces his development towards his acceptance of the *analogia entis* within the broader framework of the *analogia fidei.*[65] Urs von Balthasar's wrestling with Barth over the problem of nature and grace is not only a good example of Dialectics in practice but also shows clearly how *Method's* transposition of natural theology to within the horizon of faith is so important for opening the method to ecumenical use.[66]

Barth himself carried on a lifelong debate with the theology of Schleiermacher, and the issues of that debate have dominated much Protestant thought in this century. Lonergan's use of conversion draws him into this debate on its crucial issue, that of the point of contact between man and God. As Stephen Sykes has written: 'Something has to be pointed to as evidence; and Schleiermacher begins a whole tradition of theology by pointing to human religious experience.'[67] Rudolf Otto and Paul Tillich, who are in this tradition, are both quoted with approval by Lonergan on conversion.[68] As has been shown above, whether he escapes the criticisms aimed at other theologies which have been anchored in the data of consciousness depends on acceptance of his philosophy, which claims to do justice to God's transcendence and to the objectivity of revelation. Whatever one's judgement on this, however, it is striking how both Lonergan and Schleiermacher have reinterpreted their traditions by making explicit the same basic problem of religious epistemology. Schleiermacher saw himself as continuing the Reformation, Lonergan sees himself as developing Aquinas, but their common recognition of the subject-centred standpoint may be the best approach to ecumenical reconciliation.

How useful is the method when it is applied to specific ecumenical problems? Since it is only a method, no conclusions can be deduced from it, and in the face of fundamental disagreements it is easy to see the need for men who have a three-fold conversion, but hard to find them. *Method's* concentration on the ongoing discovery of mind, on contexts and on historicity does, however, indicate that the most important ecumenical problem for theologians is the development of doctrine.[69] So the ecumenical question to be asked of *Method* here is whether this question is prejudged. Is it possible to hold Protestant views of doctrinal development without ending up in 'counter-positions'? Professor Lindbeck in his paper, *Protestant problems with Lonergan on the development of dogma*,[70] has concluded that this is possible, and Lonergan has agreed with him.[71] Lindbeck's paper is valuable in explaining just why this is so in the specialty of doctrines, which is where the authority of his own church plays such a large part in Lonergan's thought. That study pairs with one by Lonergan's long-standing collaborator, Fr. F. E. Crowe, S.J., entitled 'Development of Doctrine: Aid or Barrier to Christian Unity?'[72]: from both sides of the fence there is the suggestion that Lonergan's approach 'can serve as a major ecumenical contribution'.[73] Yet as always, Lonergan's philosophy remains the sign outside the bracket, demanding that high level of agreement which is intellectual conversion.

A COHERENT VIEW OF THE CHRISTIAN?

This article has been mainly concerned with understanding Lonergan's present position on a few topics in relation to his earlier thought. In conclusion I would like to take the title more comprehensively and recall a remark of his about the shift to interiority being axial.[74] That is a stupendous claim, for in Karl Jasper's terminology it places the change in the same category as what happened in the emergence of the world's major religions. On this view *Method's* place in the Lonergan *corpus* is as part of a life's work devoted to realizing the potentiality of the new era, whose possibilities (including the ideal of cosmopolis) are sketched in *Insight*, Ch. VII. This view of a complex world in evolution, and of the drastic truncation produced by leaving out man's relationship to God[75] is perhaps the best way to see the unity of a life's work that has dealt with mathematics, the physical, biological and human sciences, education, history, philosophy and above all theology. Lonergan could identify himself with what he says of a contemporary Jesuit: 'It has been the great merit of Teilhard de Chardin to have recognized the Christian's need for a coherent image of himself and to have contributed not a little towards meeting that need.'[76]

NOTES

1 The best generally available bibliography is that in *The Achievement of Bernard Lonergan* by David Tracy, New York, 1970. The most complete is at the Lonergan Centre, Regis College.
2 I am very grateful to Regis College for their hospitality, and especially to Fr. F. E. Crowe for all his assistance, and to Dr. Philip McShane for giving me the benefit of his familiarity with the materials of the Centre. The tapes are in the process of being transcribed, and translations or English summaries of the Latin texts are also being produced.
3 Ed. Fr. Patout Burns, S.J., New York, 1971. First published 1941-42 as articles in *Theological Studies*. The main points are included in his

systematic work, *De ente supernaturali: Supplementum schematicum*, L'Immaculee-Conception, Montreal 1946 (unpublished). An article, 'Openness and Religious Experience' published in *Collection*, edited F. E. Crowe, New York 1967, 198-202, is very helpful in bridging the gap between *Grace and Freedom* and *Method* in the way grace is described.

4 *Insight, A Study of Human Understanding*, New York, 1970, first published London, 1957.
5 E.g. *De Constitutione Christi*, Rome, 1964. *De Deo Trino*, Rome, 1964. *De Verbo Incarnato*, Rome, 1964.
6 *Verbum. Word and Idea in Aquinas*, ed. David B. Burrell, C.S.C., London, 1968. First published 1946-49 as articles in *Theological Studies*.
7 Op. cit.
8 *Method* 107, 241.
9 *Foundations of Theology*, ed. P. McShane, Dublin, 1971, 232.
10 Lonergan Centre papers, V. 7a, V. 7c, V. 10k.
11 *Method* 123.
12 On this parallel see F. E. Crowe's review of *Method* in *Science et Esprit*, Vol. XXV, 1973.
13 *Ibid.* 121-125.
14 *Ibid.* 124.
15 *Method* 122.
16 *Grace and Freedom* 124.
17 *Method* 115.
18 *Ibid.* 115.
19 *The Clergy Review* 57 (1972) 579-596.
20 In McShane, op. cit. 194-196.
21 *The Heythrop Journal*, Vol. XIII, No. 4, October, 1972, 418-419.
22 The paragraph in which this is summed up is in the middle of 107, *Method*.
23 *Method* 96.
24 *Ibid.* 120-124. See also 288-289, 340-344. It is easier to understand how Lonergan can transpose Aquinas in this way if one notes that 'not only *sentire* and *intelligere* but also *velle* can be a *pati*'. (*Verbum* 132).
25 *Method* 120.
26 *Ibid.* 121.
27 *Ibid.* 120.
28 Op. cit. 419.
29 See a report of Lonergan's answers after a lecture in the supplementary volume: *Discussions: Congress on the theology of the renewal of the Church*, Toronto, 1968, 5-8.
30 *Ibid.* 338.
31 Op. cit. 594.
32 In McShane, op. cit. 41-59. See especially Section II.
33 See e.g. *Grace and Freedom* 93-116, *Insight* Ch. XIX, XX, and the unpublished *De Praedestinatione*, Regis College, Toronto, 1950.
34 Note too *Method* 123-124, for hints of how his view is at one with the 'older and more authoritative tradition'.
35 McShane, op. cit. 194-196.
36 For Lonergan's own Christology see the two relevant Latin works under

37 note 5. The best brief summary I have found of the place of Christ in his theology is the first two paragraphs of an unpublished Latin work, *De Bono et Malo*, 1963-1964 (Lonergan Centre, IX. 5).
37 *Method* 7, footnote. No alternative to *Insight* is suggested!
38 *Ibid.* XII.
39 *Insight* 744.
40 See *Method* 339.
41 *Ibid.* 338.
42 Cf. *The Origins of Christian Realism*, unpublished lecture at Regis College, Toronto, Sept. 8th, 1961.
43 McShane, op. cit. 72.
44 *The Modern Churchman*, I (N.S.), Oct., 1957, 143.
45 'An interview with Fr. Bernard Lonergan, S.J., by Philip McShane, S.J.', *The Clergy Review*, June, 1971, 426.
46 See *Insight*, Chs. X and XI, also 639-640.
47 *Ibid.* 675.
48 *Ibid.* 599.
49 *Ibid.* 658.
50 McShane, op. cit. 219.
51 See *Insight* 19.
52 Cf. W. Pannenberg in *Basic Questions in Theology*, Vol. II, London, 1971, 221 : 'Whether this characteristic openness of human behaviour presupposes such a supporting ground (as God), different from the entire realm of existing beings (that is to say, the world) precisely because what is being inquired into is man's openness to inquire beyond everything in existence; or whether this openness is only an expression of the self-creative power of man as an "acting being", is probably the central problem inherent in the modern idea of man's "openness to the world" or self-transcendence." Here the 'concomitant positive context' (*Insight* 24) required for an inverse insight is 'the self-creative power of man as an acting being'.
53 *Insight* 640.
54 *Method* 339.
55 *Insight* 635.
56 *Method* 116.
57 *Ibid.* 338.
58 McShane, op. cit. 4.
59 For the context of these remarks on the stages of theology both in Lonergan's works and in the history of the theology see Tracy's article in McShane, op. cit. 197-222.
60 *Method* XII.
61 *Ibid.* 119.
62 *Ibid.* 360.
63 *Ibid.* 318.
64 *The Theology of Karl Barth*, trans. by John Drury, New York, 1972.
65 Cf. op. cit. 138.
66 Another way of seeing the ecumenical significance of Lonergan's latest development is in the terms used by Otto Pesch in his monumental comparative study of justification in Luther and Aquinas, *Theologie der*

Rechtfertigung bei Martin Luther und Thomas von Aquin. Versuch eines systematisch-theologischen Dialogs, Mainz, 1967. He contrasts two styles of theology, with Aquinas as sapiential and Luther as existential. Lonergan's 'shift to interiority' offers a higher viewpoint on both styles and avoids having to choose between them by proposing a common method.
67 *Friedrich Schleiermacher,* by Stephen Sykes, London, 1971, 47.
68 *Method* 106.
69 See *Method,* Ch. XII, *passim.*
70 In McShane, op. cit. 115-123.
71 *Ibid.* 232.
72 In *Proceedings of the Catholic Theological Society of America,* Vol. 21, 1-20.
73 McShane, op. cit. 123.
74 *The Clergy Review,* June 1971, 428.
75 See Lonergan's contribution to the series *Studies in the Spirituality of Jesuits,* Vol. II, No. 3, St. Louis, Sept. 1970.
76 *Method* 315.

Knowledge, Understanding and Reality — Some Questions Concerning Lonergan's Philosophy

Patrick J. McGrath

Lonergan's project in *Insight* is expressed in the famous slogan which, in his own words, 'sums up the positive content of the work'.

> Thoroughly understand what it is to understand and not only will you understand the broad lines of all there is to be understood, but you will have a fixed base, an invariant pattern, opening upon all further developments of understanding.[1]

Two things strike one immediately on reading this — the magnitude of the claim that is being expressed and the vagueness of the language that is used to express it. It is a claim concerning all of human knowledge, concerning not merely everything that is already known, but everything that ever will or could be known. If it is true, then it could hardly avoid being extraordinarily important. But what precisely is being claimed? The terminology used is extremely vague and Lonergan, despite the importance which he attaches to this slogan, offers no further elucidation of it. What does 'the broad lines of all there is to be understood' mean, for instance? We would normally take it as referring to the essential points or basic elements of all there is to be understood, but it hardly makes sense to say that an understanding of understanding will give you an understanding of the essential points of, say, the Theory of Relativity, even if you have no previous knowledge of physics. And it makes even less sense to say that every item of human knowledge has the same set of essential points as every other — which is what Lonergan's principle would seem to imply.

In the second part of the slogan the metaphors appear to have got mixed. It is not so easy to see how an understanding of understanding could provide you with either a fixed base or an invariant pattern, but when the base or pattern is supposed to function like a door or a window and *open upon* something, then the problem of interpretation becomes difficult indeed. Why, in any event, should Lonergan have thought it necessary to introduce these two new

27

metaphors? He could have expressed his basic principle simply as: 'Thoroughly understand what it is to understand and you will understand the broad lines of all there is to be understood and of all further developments of understanding.' If this formulation does not differ in meaning from the formulation which was actually adopted by Lonergan, he would hardly have rejected it in favour of the latter. But if the two formulations are not equivalent in meaning, then it appears that an understanding of understanding will not, in Lonergan's view, provide you with the broad lines of all further developments of understanding, but with something weaker — 'a fixed base, an invariant pattern'. This position hardly makes sense, however, because Lonergan clearly looks on the structure of the act of understanding as something constant. But if this is so, then the relationship between understanding and what has already been understood will be no different from the relationship between understanding and what has not yet been, but will eventually be, understood. Thus, if an understanding of understanding will now provide you with an understanding of the broad lines of the structure of deoxryibonucleic acid, something discovered only in 1953, then an understanding of understanding would have provided you with the same insight or information in 1950, since the character of understanding has not changed in the meantime.

How then are we to explain Lonergan's actual formulation of his basic principle? He may have felt that it would be implausible to assert that an understanding of understanding would provide you with an understanding of the broad lines of all further developments of understanding and so he watered down the claim by speaking instead of 'a fixed base, an invariant pattern, opening upon all further developments'. This would account for the change in terminology, but it hardly inspires confidence in the validity of the principle. However, there does not appear to be any alternative explanation.

The air of absurdity which surrounds the principle when it is applied to concrete instances of understanding may suggest that it should be interpreted as referring not to the *content* of what is understood, but to its *form*. Thus, it could be argued that every item of human knowledge has the same general form as every other and that one can, therefore, know in advance the general form of every new development in human knowledge. But it is difficult to be sure that this is Lonergan's position and even more difficult, if this is his position, to see how it makes sense. For Lonergan's fundamental point is that an understanding of understanding will provide you with the basis for an understanding of reality as a whole or, as he himself puts it, that 'metaphysics is derived from the known structure of one's knowing'.[2] But if 'the known structure of one's knowing' concerns merely the form of human knowledge— that aspect of knowledge which is derived from the mind as opposed to that aspect which is derived from reality — what reason is there for thinking that this tells you anything about reality? One could, of course, adopt the Kantian distinction between reality as it is in itself and reality as it appears to us and argue that reality as it appears to us must necessarily conform to the structure of one's knowing. But Lonergan appears explicitly to reject this distinction in its Kantian sense.[3]

Perhaps it would be a help to interpretation if at this stage we were to enquire what sort of principle Lonergan's basic dictum is intended to be. Is it an inductive principle? Or if not, is it analytic? Or if neither of these, is it synthetic *a priori*? Oddly enough Lonergan's doesn't deal with this question, but we may, I believe, go some distance towards answering it for ourselves. It seems clear, first of all, that the principle is not intended to be analytic. An analytic proposition is one whose denial involves a contradiction, but there seems to be no contradiction involved in the denial of Lonergan's basic principle and Lonergan makes no attempt to show that there is — something that would be incomprehensible if he believed it to be analytic. The same sort of reasoning would appear to exclude the idea that the principle is to be regarded as synthetic *a priori*. A statement is a true synthetic *a priori* proposition only if its denial, though not contradictory, is somehow inconceivable. And whatever about the truth of Lonergan's principle, its falsity does not appear inconceivable, nor does he ever suggest that it is.

Is it an inductive principle, then? This is a more plausible suggestion than the others, for we can easily visualize the principle being argued for in an inductive fashion. This could be done by comparing the structure of the act of understanding with a number of items of human knowing, thereby showing, or at least endeavouring to show, that the broad lines of these different items are reflected in the structure of the act. But Lonergan himself does not adduce any such evidence and if he regarded the principle as an inductive one, he could hardly have failed to do so.

WHAT IS THE BASIC DICTUM?

Well, then, if the principle is neither inductive, nor analytic, nor synthetic *a priori*, what is it? The answer, I believe, is that it is the expression of a philosophical theory concerning the relationship between knowledge and reality. It must be admitted that, aside from the fact that it seems to be the only remaining possibility, there is little evidence one can offer in support of this view, for philosophical theories need to be supported by arguments and Lonergan leaves his basic principle, at least at the point where he formally enunciates it, devoid of argumentative support. However, at a later stage in *Insight* an argument appears which, though not specifically put forward in support of the basic principle, appears to exhibit the reasoning which underlies it. This is so brief that one can scarcely credit that an essential point would be argued in such a casual way. But at any rate it is the nearest thing to an argument in support of the principle to be found in the pages of *Insight*. It runs as follows:

> Knowing and the known, if they are not an identity, at least stand in some correspondence and, as the known is reached only through knowing, structural features of the one are bound to be reflected in the other.[4]

This argument is not itself sufficient to establish the truth of Lonergan's principle, for even if there is an isomorphism between knowing and the known, it may be too slight to warrant the claim that a knowledge of the structure of knowing or understanding will provide you with a knowledge of the broad lines of all there is to be known or understood. However, if the argument is sound, it would certainly go a considerable distance towards showing that Lonergan's basic principle is correct.

But is the argument sound? What it says is that since the known is reached only through knowing, structural features of the one are bound to be reflected in the other. But why should the fact that A is reached only through B mean that A and B must have structural features in common? When stated thus in general terms, the reasoning does not seem at all plausible. But perhaps this is to distort the argument, for Lonergan may be using the term 'reach' in a special sense. If he is, however, he hasn't told us so. 'Reach' is one of these elusive metaphorical terms which Lonergan is fond of employing but not of elucidating. Nevertheless he may be using it here to refer exclusively to the special way in which through knowing one 'reaches' that which is known. But if so, then the statement 'The known is reached only through knowing' is equivalent to 'The known is reached in the manner exclusive to knowing only through knowing'; and this is a vacuous statement, a tautology which could not form the basis for any significant conclusion. If, on the other hand, 'reach' is being used in the ordinary sense of 'to make contact with', then the statement is equivalent to 'We make contact with the known only through knowing'. And this is to render the statement false, for we have contact with reality in all sorts of ways other than by knowing it.

Could the term 'only' not be omitted from the argument and this difficulty thus avoided? Perhaps the best way to answer this question is by raising another: Why was 'only' inserted in the argument in the first place? For Lonergan's point is surely that as the known is reached through knowing, there must be an isomorphism between the two. If there were other ways of reaching the known apart from knowing, this would not detract from the necessity for an isomorphism between knowing and the known. But why then was the word 'only' ever inserted in the premise? The answer in my opinion is that if it were omitted, then the conclusion of the argument would be that there is an isomorphism not merely between knowing and the known, but between the known and any human activity which puts us in contact with it. And this, to say the least, sounds implausible — or it could be made plausible only by rendering the isomorphism so weak as to be of no account. To avoid this awkward consequence the word 'only' has to be inserted. But the premise is thereby rendered either tautologous or false.

REFORMULATION?

Clearly, Lonergan's argument as it stands has little or nothing to be said for it. But it may be premature to dismiss it immediately as worthless, for the argument can, I believe, be reformulated in such a way as to avoid the difficulties which I have urged against it. The reformulated version runs as follows: Unless there is an isomorphism between knowing and the known, reality would be unknowable. But it is not unknowable. Therefore, this isomorphism must exist.

What are we to make of this? The crucial point is obviously the truth of the major premise. Why should the lack of an isomorphism between knowing and reality render reality unknowable? One reason why someone might be inclined to think this is that human knowledge must, in some sense, mirror reality; therefore there must be a structure common to the two. But to say that there must be a structure common to knowledge and reality is not at all the same thing as to say that there must be an isomorphism between knowing or understanding and reality — just as to say that there must be an isomorphism between a photograph and its object is not to say that there must be an isomorphism between the object photographed and the operation of the photographic mechanism. Knowledge is one thing, knowing is something else.

Why should it be thought then that there must be an isomorphism between knowing and the known for reality to be knowable? Perhaps the most plausible reason is this: The human cognitive faculties are not passive agencies which simply mirror reality; rather they actively organize the data presented to them. Thus, what is seen is organized in a way characteristic of the sense of vision; what is heard is organized in a way characteristic of the sense of hearing and so on. This is equally true of knowing or understanding. Our knowledge is organized in a way that is characteristic of human intelligence and in that sense there is an isomorphism between the known and our manner of knowing it. However, this is not something inherent in the known, but rather is imposed on it by the cognitive faculty. What is inherent in the known is merely the capacity to be organized in this way. In that very qualified sense then there is an isomorphism between knowing and the known, but it would appear to be much too weak a sense for Lonergan's purpose. For to say that reality is knowable only if the data it supplies to the mind is capable of being organized in the manner characteristic of human knowing is to say very little, perhaps nothing at all. What would it mean to say that the data supplied by reality are incapable of being thus organized — that, say, reality is incapable of being described by means of universal terms. If such a supposition is meaningless — and I suspect that it is, seeing that you cannot even express it without applying certain universal terms to reality — then to say that the data supplied by reality have the capacity to be organized in the manner characteristic of human knowing is to say nothing at all. Even if this is not so, it would appear to be much too slender a basis for the claim that if we understand what it is to understand, we will understand the broad lines of all there is to be understood.

KNOWING UNDERSTANDING AND INSIGHT

So far I have been concerned with the meaning of Lonergan's basic principle and the reasons for believing it to be true. I now wish to examine its significance for Lonergan's philosophy as expounded in *Insight*. The principle, as we have seen, is concerned with understanding. This concept is central to the entire work. Two other related concepts seem equally central and important. These are the concepts of knowing and insight. Now at this stage we come across a strange lacuna in *Insight* — that even though we are told that the main purpose of the book is to enable us to know what it is to know, to understand what it is to understand, to gain an insight into insight, there is in fact no attempt made to analyse these terms or to examine their meaning or to work out their relationship to other terms. Lonergan has failed, in other words, to engage in even the most elementary conceptual analysis for the central concepts of his philosophy.

There is, however, a fairly obvious answer to this charge. What could be more familiar to us, it might be asked, than knowing or understanding or having an insight? As Thomas Reid said in reply to Hume: 'To a man that understands English, there are surely no words that require explanation less.'[5] We all know perfectly what they mean, so why waste time with a tedious explanation or examination of them. This is certainly true, but as an answer to the charge it is unsatisfactory. For it is one thing to know what a term means; it is quite a different matter to give a correct account of its meaning. Or to put this in a slightly different way — it is one thing to be able to use a concept correctly in making judgments; it is quite another to be able to give a correct account of its use. We all know what the word 'true' or the word 'good' means, for example, but we would be in immediate difficulties if someone were to ask us for an account of their meaning. Nor is this surprising, seeing that philosophers have been in disagreement about these concepts for centuries. But the important point is that while in the ordinary course of events we don't need to be able to give a correct account of these concepts to be able to use them to make true judgments —

it is sufficient to know what they mean simply — this is not true at the philosophical level. Philosophy is a second order activity in the sense that the philosopher is concerned not — or at least not solely — to make true judgments by means of philosophical concepts, but rather true judgments about them; hence it is necessary for him not merely to know how to use such concepts, but also to be clear on how they are to be used. Otherwise confusion is almost certain to occur.

It appears to me that by failing to engage in the sort of linguistic or conceptual analysis I have mentioned, Lonergan has misunderstood the character of the basic concepts of his philosophy. To illustrate this point I will quote two short passages — the first from *Insight*, the second from *Method in Theology*.

> The present work falls into two parts. . . . The first part deals with the question, What is happening when we are knowing? The second deals with the question, What is known when that is happening? (p. XXII).

> Transcendental method . . . brings to light our conscious and intentional operations and thereby leads to answers to three basic questions. What am I doing when I am knowing? Why is doing that knowing? What do I know when I do it? (p. 25).

I do not believe that anyone who had examined the concept of knowing could have written either of these two passages. They appear to me to constitute a typical example of what Wittgenstein had in mind in writing,

> when we do philosophy we are like savages, primitive people, who hear the expressions of civilized men, put a false interpretation on them, and then draw the queerest conclusions from it.[6]

Wittgenstein does not mean, presumably, that this always happens when we do philosophy, but that it is always liable to happen. For when we do philosophy, language, as he puts it, goes on holiday, that is to say, words and expressions are taken from the context in which they are normally used and placed in a highly artificial philosophical context where they may easily be misinterpreted. Now in the two passages which I have just quoted from Lonergan, the word 'known' has clearly lost its way while on holiday, for we never use it as Lonergan has used it here. Take the question 'What is happening when we are knowing?' Do we ever speak in this way? Would we ever say, for example, 'When I was knowing Pythagoras's theorem, the telephone rang'? The answer, clearly, is that we wouldn't. And this is not just a matter of linguistic convention. We don't speak in this way because, if we did, our remarks would be devoid of sense. If someone were to say 'When I was knowing Pythagoras's theorem, the telephone rang', we would immediately conclude that either he had inadvertently used the word 'knowing' for a word such as 'studying' or 'learning' or that he was a foreigner whose knowledge of English was defective. Or take the first line of the poem 'The Lake Isle of Innisfree' — 'I will arise and go now'. Yeats couldn't have written 'I will arise and know now', for if he had, he would have been uttering nonsense. But if knowing is doing something, Lonergan asserts, there would be no reason why one shouldn't arise and do it.

This sort of misunderstanding of the character of the concepts of 'knowing', 'understanding' and 'insight' occurs frequently in Lonergan's work. For example he speaks of insight as an activity (*Insight*, p. X) and elsewhere as an event (p. XXII). And he also speaks of 'conveying an insight' (p. IX) and of 'having an insight' (p. 3). But while you can observe an event, you cannot have it; and while you can perform an activity, you cannot convey it. Here again there has been a misinterpretation of the character of a concept. In other places Lonergan appears to identify knowing and understanding. Again, this sort of error could hardly survive an examination of the use of these terms. To say that you know someone is not to say that you understand him; and to say that you understand a proposition is not to claim that you know that it is true. Knowing and understanding are closely related, but not identical.

How important is all this? I would not wish to claim that all the points I have made are of great importance for an evaluation of Lonergan's philosophy. Some of them are perhaps of no great significance in themselves. But they are symptoms of something which is significant — namely, that Lonergan appears to have misunderstood the character of the concepts which are central to his philosophy. And this must raise serious doubts about the validity of the entire enterprise.

PRESUPPOSITIONS CONCERNING UNDERSTANDING

The purpose of the enterprise is to provide us with an understanding of understanding, an account of the dynamic structure of the act of understanding. This involves two presuppositions about understanding — and indeed about knowing and insight as well, but in the interest of simplicity I will concentrate on understanding. Both these presuppositions are apparently accepted by Lonergan without examination or argument. The first is that understanding is a uniform activity, that it is something like walking or typing or climbing except, of course, that it occurs in the mind. Whenever you engage in walking or typing, you always do more or less the same sort of thing. So it would, I suppose, make sense to refer to the 'dynamic structure' of the act of walking or typing, though it is difficult to see what is the point of the word 'dynamic' here, since the structure of an act is presumably dynamic by definition.

There are, however, other human activities such as working, housekeeping, gardening, to which this sort of terminology does not apply. We do not speak of an act of working or an act of housekeeping or an act of gardening, for what each of these terms refers to is not a specific activity, but a whole range of diverse activities. There would be no sense, therefore, in enquiring into the dynamic structure of the act of housekeeping for there is no such thing, though one could perhaps enquire into the different dynamic structures of the various acts which come under the generic title of housekeeping such as cooking, cleaning, dusting or washing-up. Now understanding would appear to be far more akin to working or gardening or housekeeping than it is to walking or climbing or typing. The mental activities associated with understanding would appear to be as many and as diverse as the different types of problem and different sorts of subject matter to which the human mind applies itself. Think of the difference between understanding a word and understanding a sentence — a sentence can usually be understood the first time you encounter it whereas a new word has to be explained — between understanding a language and understanding a work of art — acquiring an understanding of a language is largely a matter of memory, but memory only plays a minimal rôle in understanding a work of art — between understanding a subject like philosophy and understanding a person. I do not see how anyone who contrasts these different instances of understanding could seriously take the view that there is a uniform mental activity associated with understanding which has a specific dynamic structure.

Lonergan's second presupposition about understanding is that it is an act. He constantly refers to it as such. The phrase 'an act of understanding' occurs twenty-four times in the first hundred pages of *Insight*. (He also refers, though not so frequently, to acts of knowing and acts of insight.) This second presupposition is, I believe, as unwarranted as the first. There are no such things as acts of understanding. In saying this I am not, however, making a statement of empirical fact — it isn't as if I had ransacked my mind and discovered no traces there of acts of understanding; it is a question rather of the impossibility of assigning any coherent meaning to the phrase 'act of understanding'. Modern linguistic philosophy has familiarised us with the idea that in discussing philosophical problems we may utter remarks which, while impeccable from the point of view of grammar or syntax, turn out on closer examination to be devoid of sense. Various, though not necessarily conflicting, explanations have been offered as to how this occurs. Bertrand Russell believes that there are different levels of language and that to use a second order concept as if it were a first order one or vice versa will produce absurdity. Gilbert Ryle attributes the meaninglessness which occurs in philosophical discussion to a confusion between different logical categories, while Wittgenstein in his later writings thinks that it is brought about by failure to advert to the differences between different language games. What all these explanations have in common is the idea that philosophers sometimes lapse into incoherence by using terms or expressions in a way that is quite alien to the way they are used in the ordinary non-philosophical contexts which are their original home.

This error seems to me to vitiate Lonergan's treatment of the concepts which are central to his whole enterprise. For in non-philosophical contexts we never speak of understanding or knowing or having an insight as acts. This point can be brought out in a number of ways. (Again I will concentrate on understanding, but the same arguments apply to the other two concepts.)

1. If understanding were an act, it should cease when the mind temporarily ceases to function or when it is concerned with some other topics. But this is not so. A mathematician does not cease

to understand differential calculus when he is asleep nor does a polygot cease to understand other languages when he is speaking or reading English.

2. Actions occur at a certain point of time and they endure for a certain period of time. We say 'I was reading or typing or daydreaming when the telephone rang' or 'I spent half an hour reading or typing or daydreaming this morning', but it makes no sense to say 'I was understanding Pythagoras's theorem when the telephone rang' or 'I spent half an hour understanding Pythagoras's theorem this morning'.

3. If understanding were act, then it should make sense to speak of deciding to do it. But this is not the case. We may indeed speak of deciding to study some topic or deciding to try to understand it, but if someone were to say 'I have decided to understand the causes of the English Civil War', we would immediately convict him of misuse of words.

But if understanding is not an act, then what is it? This is not necessarily a question to which there is a proper answer, for in asking it, what one is seeking is a category, such as 'act' or 'process', which was originally used for describing the physical world and then applied in a somewhat extended sense to the world of minds; and it may well be that there is not such category available which would be suitable for explaining the nature of understanding. Like God, understanding may be such that it is possible to say what it is not, but not what it is. However, I do not think that the situation is quite so desperate as that. If we are asked 'What is understanding?', the correct answer, I believe, is that it is a state of mind. This answer is, however, open to a number of misinterpretations. If we treat understanding as a state of mind, we may be tempted to assimilate it to a certain type of mental state such as a feeling of fear or a sensation of pain. This would be a mistake for two reasons. A feeling or sensation is a conscious state of mind — one cannot have a feeling of fear or a sensation of pain without being aware of it. But not all states of mind are conscious states. One can be habitually afraid of something, e.g. travelling by air, without being always conscious of it and to say that one is in love with someone does not imply that one is always conscious of one's love.

Now understanding, as is clear from our discussion of the phrase 'an act of understanding', is an habitual state of mind rather than a state which is present only so long as one is conscious of it. So to say that one understands something is to assert the existence of a state of mind, but it is not necessarily to say anything about what is passing through one's mind at this moment.

Secondly, a feeling or internal sensation is wholly internal to the mind of the individual who is the subject of it, but understanding is not. This may appear surprising, since we are inclined to take for granted that a state is always wholly internal to the thing of which it is a state, but in fact not all states are of this kind. The state of being married, for instance, is not wholly internal to the married person, since it depends on another person to whom he or she is married. And in mental states too you find some which are wholly internal to the mind and others which are not. Belief, for example, is a wholly internal mental state whereas knowledge is not. This arises from the fact that the question of what you believe is entirely a matter of your internal state of mind, whereas the question of what you know cannot be answered by reference to your mind alone, but depends also on the way things are. It makes no sense to speak of knowing what is false; hence to say that one knows that it is raining implies something about one's internal state of mind and something about the state of the weather. Now understanding is more like knowing than believing in the sense that it, too, is not wholly internal to the mind of the person who understands. 'Understanding' as it is normally used, is an 'achievement word' in that it implies success. You do not understand something unless you have *correctly* grasped the nature of the thing any more than you do not know something unless what you know is true. Thus, it would make no sense to speak of someone understanding my motives if he had a completely wrong idea of what my motives are. The question of whether you understand something cannot be resolved, therefore, by reference to your mind alone; one must also take account of the character of what is said to be understood.

Now in *Insight* Lonergan, under the influence of the idea that understanding is an act, assumes throughout that one acquires an understanding of understanding through introspection.

> The dynamic, cognitional structure to be reached is not the transcendental *ego* of Fichtean speculation, nor the abstract

pattern of relations verifiable in Tom and Dick and Harry, but the personally appropriated structure of one's own experiencing, one's own intelligent inquiry and insights, one's own critical reflection and judging and deciding. The crucial issue is an experimental issue, and the experiment will be performed not publicly but privately. It will consist in one's own rational self-consciousness clearly and distinctly taking possession of itself as rational self-consciousness. Up to that decisive achievement, all leads. From it, all follows.[7]

But if understanding is a mental state of the type we have described, then there would appear to be insuperable difficulties in the view that its nature can be grasped by introspection. The first difficulty is that since understanding is not wholly internal to the mind, it cannot be fully grasped by mental inspection; indeed introspection can give no guarantee that what is being examined is a genuine instance of understanding, since this depends as much on the character of what is understood as on the internal state of mind of the person who understands. Secondly, since understanding is not a conscious state of mind, it does not appear susceptible to examination by introspective methods. It may seem odd to speak of understanding as a non-conscious state of mind, but while one may be conscious *that* one understands, one cannot be conscious *of* one's understanding in the same way as one can be conscious of thinking or day-dreaming. This point may be substantiated in a number of ways. Firstly, if understanding were a conscious state, it should cease when one ceases to be conscious or even when one ceases to be conscious of the object of understanding; and this is obviously untrue. Secondly, if understanding were a state of mind that is susceptible to introspective examination, we could never really be in doubt as to whether one understands something or not — just as one cannot be in doubt as to whether one is thinking of something or not — but this is a point about which we are not merely frequently in doubt, but often in error. Lastly, consider what it means to examine a particular instance of understanding — one's understanding of, say, the French Revolution or the twentieth-century novel. To examine your understanding of the French Revolution is to do nothing more than to consider the French Revolution. It is to ask yourself such questions as 'Is this what really happened?', 'Is this the correct explanation for the events in question?' Clearly these could not be answered by recourse to introspection.

There are, of course, certain mental acts associated with understanding, such as thinking, pondering, calculating, which are to some extent open to introspective examination. But to examine these introspectively is not to examine understanding for the reason that one may do all these things and not understand or, alternatively, we may understand without having done any of them, as in the case of infused understanding. (Whether infused understanding is a reality is irrelevant here; all that matters is that there appears to be no reason for thinking it to be logically impossible.) Introspection may tell you something about the workings of the human mind, therefore, but this is a different thing from claiming that it gives you an insight into the invariant structure of understanding.

Finally, I would like to raise a comprehensive difficulty concerning Lonergan's appeal to introspection. The use of introspection as a means of acquiring an insight into the invariant structure of understanding depends for its validity on understanding being the same for everyone; otherwise introspection will reveal nothing more than details of purely autobiographical interest. But how could Lonergan *know* that understanding has an invariant structure which is the same for all if we are dependent on introspection for our knowledge of understanding? In other words, Lonergan's method makes no sense unless he already knows a great deal about how others understand. And this knowledge could not have been gained from introspection.

NOTES

1 *Insight* XXVIII.
2 *Ibid.* XXIX.
3 Cf. *Ibid.* 339-342.
4 *Ibid.* 115.
5 *Essays on the Active Powers of Man*, V, VII. Reid was here discussing the meaning of 'ought' and 'ought not'.
6 *Philosophical Investigations*, paragraph 194.
7 *Insight* XVIII.

Lonergan's Notion of Being in Relation to His 'Method'

Noel Dermot O'Donoghue, O.D.C.

THE TWO CLASSICAL STANDPOINTS

Those who try to think about reality comprehensively and systematically do so either from the standpoint of reality or from the standpoint of thought, and this standpoint is, as a rule, a starting-point also, and a point of reference. Everything is seen from this point of view, that is to say in terms of relation to a reality 'given' or presented to the mind, or in terms of relation to the thinking subject; everything is related to this as to a central unchanging point of reference. When one switches from a writer who takes the one standpoint to one who takes the other, one has to make a change analogous to that by which one sees a chessboard as white on black rather than black on white. Perhaps a good part of the disagreements among philosophers arises from the refusal on both sides to make this change of mental focus, though the question may still be asked as to which standpoint provides the more logical and comprehensive account of reality. Of course, every system of philosophy worth the name will take both poles into account, but one standpoint will always remain primary, and the system will take its whole shape from this.

In other words, every philosophical system is either ontological in standpoint or epistemological.

Most of the great philosophical systems of the West have been ontological. Aristotelianism in its original and in its medieval forms, the systems of Spinoza and Leibnitz are obvious examples. But Platonism is also an ontological system, for Plato's standpoint is that of the 'really real' (*to ontōs on*) — his theory of Ideas arises not from the point of view of an analysis of knowledge, but from the side of a clear apprehension of the physical world as changeable (and therefore not 'really real'), an apprehension that leads him to seek the real in a world open to intelligence. It is the object that concerns him, not the subject. We miss the whole concern of his thinking if we see him as the philosopher of the Ideas considered as the objects of intelligence; he is all the way concerned with reality and realities. The *Republic* is not primarily concerned with the idea of Justice but with the reality of Justice, and this is true of all those matters with which he is seriously concerned. His concern is with reality, and this is true of all the great Platonists, Plotinus and Augustine, for example, as it is also true of a contemporary Platonist such as Sciacca. Descartes was also an ontological thinker: his concern is not with the *cognito* but with the *sum* — the reality of thought reveals the reality of the self. And here it is worth noting that it is one thing to examine thought as *thought* and quite a different thing to examine thought as *reality*. This latter approach is that of Descartes and of all those philosophers who have been directly inspired by his thinking.

Berkeley might at first sight seem the very type of the epistemological philosopher, yet no philosopher tells us more plainly that his concern and his standpoint is ontological. ' 'Tis on the Discovering of the nature and meaning and import of Existence that I chiefly insist', he tells us in the *Philosophical Commentaries,* and this primacy of ontological concern is reiterated in the *Treatise* and elsewhere.[1] Berkeley was concerned with *esse* rather than *percipi*, with reality rather than thought. Reality is both his standpoint and his point of reference. And, if we accept the relevance here of the scholastic dictum that the first in the order of intention is the last in the order of execution, it can also be said that reality was Berkeley's point of departure.

The change comes with Kant, the shift from the ontological to the epistemological pole. Previous philosophers did, of course, deal with epistemological questions such as the relativity of perception and the problem of universal ideas, but such discussions were related to a central intuition of reality, Platonic or whatever, by which the mind and its activities were judged. Kant was the first to see the whole philosophical enterprise of systematic comprehension from the standpoint of the subject, precisely as thinking and experiencing. He was quite right in seeing himself as inaugurating a 'Copernican revolution', a polar shift by which all philosophical problems were seen in a new perspective. There is still a certain polar tension in Kant's system — the 'thing in itself' resists the magnetism of the subjective pole: it is *in itself*, unrelativised, yet it is a shaded reality, homeless, outside the range of the light whose source is the subject.

This tension disappears in Hegelianism; the Copernican revolution is complete; the 'thing in itself' is reduced to ideal terms. Where Berkeley saw the reality of matter as ideal *reality* (precisely because he was concerned with reality) Hegel sees it as having its status fully accounted for in ideality as such. 'Matter', he tells us, 'is the abstract form, the existence reflected in itself, as abstract denominations, of that which is the essence of body.'[2] He is concerned not with the reality status of matter but with its ideal status, its place in a system of ideas. Phenomenology and Existentialism are based on the acceptance of the Kantian polar shift. When Husserl announces his programme of examining 'the facts themselves', the facts with which he is concerned are all subjective facts; equally the Existentialist analysis of the structures of *Dasein* encloses reality within the human subject. The empiricist philosophies have not escaped the Kantian presupposition: the Principle of Verification is (or was) an attempt to fit reality into a special scientific way of thinking about reality; it dismissed as meaningless every attempt to grapple with reality *as reality*. Linguistic analysis is, insofar as it has any philosophical relevance, an analysis of our ways of thinking: its centre of reference is the language-using subject.

There are, of course, exceptions, large and small, to the general acceptance of the Kantian revolution. The older perspective still has its adherents, not all by any means reactionaries. Latter-day scholastics such as Maritain, Gilson, De Raeymaeker, Van Steenberghen, De Lubac, Fabro, have 'retrieved' the older tradition creatively and constructively, and one has only to look at some of the dozen or so scholarly journals which continue this tradition to see that it is very much alive. Even within the world of the Kantian revolution there have been significant attempts to reverse the polar shift. The later work of Heidegger is a series of attempts to break out of the circle of subjectivity, to say something about reality as reality. We find a similar movement in the later writings of Merleau-Ponty and Jean Nabert.

On the other hand, there have been some notable attempts to find a place for the older tradition within the Kantian perspective. Maréchal made this attempt half a century ago, and, in recent times, Karl Rahner, in his early (and basic) philosophical writings has tried to situate Thomism in relation to the post-Kantian idealist perspective. The spirit and atmosphere of Rahner's enterprise is strikingly apparent in the theological encyclopedia which he has inspired, *Sacramentum Mundi,* especially in the treatment of those topics involving the rational foundations of the theology. By contrast the contemporary *Dictionary of Catholic Theology* is situated squarely within the older perspective.

It is against this background, and in relation to this polar tension that the philosophical and theological position of Bernard Lonergan is significant, fruitful and questionable.

LONERGAN'S STANDPOINT

Lonergan follows Maréchal in accepting the Kantian polar shift from object to subject. The knowing subject is his starting-point, standpoint and centre of reference. Insofar as he concerns himself with the *a priori* conditions of human knowing while maintaining the link with the traditional philosophy of the Catholic Church he may be described as a 'transcendental Thomist', and he has obviously much in common with 'transcendentalists' such as Rahner and Coreth. Where Rahner discovers the *a priori* within the pre-apprehension of being and Coreth within the activity of asking questions, Lonergan applies himself to an analysis of insight and related cognitive activities, and explores in a detailed and suggestive fashion what is involved in these activities, the necessary *a priori* conditions of their possibility. Like the other 'transcendentalists' he makes use of the method of retorsion by which counter-positions are shown to involve the very position which they deny. This method goes back to Aristotle who uses it to confute those who would deny the principle of non-contradiction. In itself the method is, it seems to me, incontrovertible, though it can be abused, and I think Lonergan does abuse it in *Method in Theology*.

But what is original and individual in Lonergan's system is his reduplication of the process of knowing. He is not content simply to explore and thematise the *a priori* conditions of knowing; this exploration is seen as itself a process of self-possession and self-appropriation. The knower whom Lonergan takes by the hand is asked to engage in the task of knowing himself, bringing to his assistance all those various mental activities which gradually reveal themselves. So it is that Lonergan keeps on assuring us that the work of interior exploration in which we are being invited to engage is not just an inward looking, not a matter of 'taking a look', however intensively and extensively, at what goes on in our minds.

Rather is it a dynamic process, doubly dynamic, for not only is knowing a dynamism but the process of knowing our knowing is also dynamic, so that a kind of intellectual laser beam is generated.

This is an exciting prospect, and it is no wonder that it sometimes leads to a hortatory and even prophetic style of writing. It perhaps explains the emergence of 'conversion' as a key notion in Lonergan's later writing. *Insight* is not so much a book as a way of life. 'The process of self-appropriation occurs only slowly, and usually, only through a struggle with some such book as *Insight*.'[3] Through this struggle one achieves 'intellectual conversion', and this is essentially bound up with moral and religious conversions. All three conversions are moments of self-transcendence achieved through ever-deepening self-appropriation.[4]

Method in Theology is the application of the theory of self-appropriation set forth in *Insight* to the special and supreme case of theological cognition. This means that the field of study is not, at least directly, theology but the mind of the theologian, or, more exactly, the human mind as theological. The function of method is 'to advert to the fact that theologies are produced by theologians, that the theologians have minds and use them, that their doing so should not be ignored or passed over but explicitly acknowledged in itself and in its implications.'[5] It is true that this is but the formal element in theological method; it has to be completed by its application to revelation and doctrine. Yet it must not be forgotten that for Lonergan the whole enterprise of theological cognition hinges on the three 'conversions' (intellectual, moral and religious), and these are achievements of self-appropriation, the unfolding of interior dynamisms by which the subject transcends itself.

The question that arises at this point (and, indeed, from the beginning, but it becomes more acute as the process of self-appropriation unfolds) is whether self-appropriation is also appropriation of reality. Are we, perhaps, like the Lady of Shalott, weaving a web of fantasy while looking at reality in a mirror? We begin with ourselves, with the knowing subject, and it would seem that the subject is at least real. But how can we tell that it is real, and what is its status as reality, whether, for instance it is absolute or relative? We are, in other words, looking for a concept or idea of reality, and we turn eagerly to those parts of his writings where Lonergan deals with this.

THE NOTION OF BEING

For Lonergan the notion of being is prior to all thinking.[6] He means, I take it, that the notion is prior to any particular exercise of thinking, for he goes on to say that the notion of being is immanent in all thinking. It is 'the immanent, dynamic orientation of cognitional process'.[7] It expresses, in fact, the basic dynamism of cognition, and is defined as 'the objective of the pure desire to know'.[8] This objective embraces 'whatever one intelligently grasps and reasonably affirms'.[9] Presumably, then, the reality of the self is assured, for the process of self-appropriation is an intelligent and reasonable process. It would seem that though Lonergan's standpoint is the subjective pole of the being-knowing polarity, yet this standpoint involves from the outset a full acceptance of the objective pole in itself and not simply as a reflection or correlative of the subjective pole. Lonergan has succeeded in the task undertaken by Maréchal, the task of accepting the Kantian polar shift and yet affirming the centrality of the objective pole.[10]

Being, then, is not an object but an objective, not a horizon of apprehension but the horizon of appetition. However, the appetition in question is not appetition in general but intellectual appetition. But is intellectual appetition possible apart from an intellected object? Lonergan thinks it is, and this is the crux of the matter. He writes:

> The desire to know is conscious intelligently and rationally; it is inquiring intelligence and reflecting reasonableness. Simply as desire, it is orientation, without as yet involving any cognitional content or notion. Still, intelligence, as obverse, looks for the intelligible as reverse. Reasonableness, as obverse, looks for the grounded, as reverse. More fundamentally, the looking for, the desiring, the inquiring-and-reflecting is an obverse that intelligently and rationally heads for an unrestricted objective named being. Were that heading unconscious, there would be an orientation towards being but there would be no desire to know being and no notion of being.[11]

What Lonergan is saying here seems to be verified by common experience. We are conscious of the fact that we have the desire to know more than we do know, that the desire for knowledge runs ahead of knowledge and draws knowledge along after it. But this desire in turn, depends on knowledge, on our general knowledge of truth and reality. We do know what we are seeking, a fuller, larger, more explicit truth, a deeper, more exact apprehension of reality. Without this the desire to know would not be an *intellectual* dynamism. What Lonergan is asking us to accept is an intellectual dynamism without 'any cognitional content or notion', presumably not even the most vague, general, abstract content or notion. And what are we to make of the claim that 'the intelligence as obverse looks to the intelligible as reverse'. Surely 'the intelligible' must mean 'intelligible reality'; otherwise the intelligible simply dissolves, and with it the intellectual dynamism. But if the intelligible looks to intelligible reality, then being is already present to intelligence as an object. It is true that being is also seen as an objective, but it is an object before it is an objective. This is true of every rational objective; it is first apprehended as an object; that is why it is rational.

Let us look at another notion which Lonergan uses in explaining and defending his notion of being, that of intentionality. This notion becomes central in *Method in Theology*. 'Intending' is seen as 'the intermediary between ignorance and knowledge'. 'What is intended is an unknown that is to be known.' [12] The notion of being intends everything; as a transcendental notion 'it constitutes the very dynamism of our conscious intending'.[13] The word 'intending' is a useful one in this context for it can be used both of apprehension and appetition, cognitively and purposively. In ordinary usage it is a purposive term ('I intend to go for a walk'). The scholastics used the term *intentio* as a cognitional term; the *intentio mentis* was the the mind's activity of apprehending an object; Brentano took it over from the scholastics, and Husserl from Brentano, so that now it is a technical philosophical term with both scholastic and phenomenological overtones. Lonergan combines the two uses of the term when he speaks of 'intentional consciousness' as open both to cognitive experience and moral and religious values.[14] At the moral level a man is responsible for what he 'intends'; moral decision is the fourth level of intentional consciousness.[15]

It may be remarked in passing that if intending is an intermediary between ignorance and knowledge it is not easy to see experiencing, understanding, judging and deciding as levels of intending, but I am rather concerned here with the ambiguity of the term 'intending' and its correlative 'intentional consciousness' as used throughout

Method in Theology, and the bearing of this ambiguity on the notion of being. If being is what we intend, it is easy to see being as an objective, for we ordinarily see objectives as the goal of intentions. But if we insist on understanding intending and intentionality in the technical cognitive sense, then being is primarily and properly an object and not an objective. It is the object of the intellect, not the objective of the will.

But why not include both intellectual and volitional activities under the blanket term of 'intentional consciousness'? And why not see being rather as the objective of the will rather than the object of intellect? Is this, perhaps, after all, what Lonergan means?

INTELLECT AND WILL

Lonergan deals explicitly with this traditional distinction in a section in *Method in Theology*, rather curiously entitled 'A Technical Note'. He rejects the distinction as part of an outmoded 'faculty psychology', and gives some reasons for doing so. At his best, as in 'Metaphysics as Horizon' Lonergan shows himself an excellent critic; at his worst he can be very bad indeed, criticising not positions but his own incredibly naïve distortions of positions. Here he sees the distinction between intellect and will as 'the notion of pure intellect or pure reason that operates on its own without guidance or control from responsible decision; and the notion of will as an arbitrary power indifferently choosing between good and evil'.[16] One is left wondering who has ever advanced these fantastic notions. It is only necessary to read a few pages dealing with this distinction in the writings of any of the great scholastic or modern authors who accept the distinction to understand that the two powers are seen as delicately interwoven and mutually co-operative and interdependent.

In fact Lonergan goes on to discuss a scholastic dictum which expresses one of the many aspects of this interdependence: *nihil amatum nisi praecognitum*, nothing is loved until it is known.[17] The more usual and general form of the dictum is *nihil volitum nisi praecognitum*, knowledge preceds will, and it is in this form especially that it poses the crucial question to Lonergan's notion of being. He does not, however, deny it, but translates it into his own system of intentional structure. 'The truth of this tag is the fact that ordinarily operations on the fourth level of intentional consciousness presuppose and complement corresponding operations on the other three'.[18] But if will is not already operative at the first three levels of consciousness (experiencing, understanding and judging) how explain their dynamic character? Both in ordinary cognition and in the notion of being it is the question of dynamism that is crucial. If knowledge precedes will, and if will is the dynamism of consciousness, how can we have a dynamism which precedes knowledge, a thrust that is at once blind, because it precedes knowledge, and intelligent because it is precisely a cognitional dynamism? Or, again, how can we have a notion of being which strives towards an objective which is not apprehended as an object?

The truth is that if one takes the subjective standpoint, seeing the knowing subject as the point of reference, there is no way of breaking through into reality. One can, of course, begin with the subject as primary *reality*, but this is to give the primacy to being. Or one can look for something *in* the subject which is real, independently of knowledge. This is the will, the dynamic orientation of the personality towards reality. Reason as practical, as directive of the will and human activities shares in this transcendence. This was the route that Kant followed, and it seems to me that in the last analysis Lonergan takes the same route. It is the dynamism of the will that gives its movement to the whole process of self-appropriation. The notion of being as the objective of the pure desire to know is not a notion at all, but simply the dynamism of the will in movement towards the good.

SUBJECT AND OBJECT

For Lonergan the process of self-appropriation is a subjective process, something in the mind, to the mind, by the mind. It is an enlarging and heightening of consciousness by a return to the self that is not mere introspection but a vital dynamic process, a process in which the operations as intentional are applied to the operations as conscious.[19] It is by way of this, and not by way of looking outwards to a world of given objects that the subject attains reality and 'objectivity'. Lonergan admits an immediate relationship to a world presented through ordinary sense experience, but he regards this contact with reality as 'elementary', as pre-critical, pre-philosophical. The reality which philosophy encounters and affirms is the reality of a world mediated by meaning, mediated by cognitional structure. At this level there is no such thing as bare objectivity; it is through the development of its own powers that the subject encounters reality. This theory of knowledge Lonergan terms 'critical realism'; it might more accurately be termed 'mediate realism', especially as the former term has been used to denote theories of knowledge rather different from that of Lonergan.

It might seem that Lonergan's critical realism is really a form of Kantian idealism, that the world mediated by meaning is simply another name for the world mediated by the *a priori* structures of the subject. But, for Lonergan, the subject opens out to an objective reality through the notion of being, which is a dynamic thrust towards reality, the revelation of a horizon within which all affirmations of reality have their place. It may be objected that the horizon is, after all, a subjective fabrication, but this would be to miss Lonergan's point that the subject is dynamically self-transcendent. The pure desire to know is unrestricted, and opens out to the plenitude of reality, transcending, therefore the limits of the finite subject. So it is that being, as the objective of the pure desire to know, is a trans-subjective horizon.

Those who take the standpoint of the object are, for Lonergan, naïve realists, who are not so much mistaken as superficial. The 'extroverted consciousness' is simply an elementary stage in the growth of man's encounter with reality. In fact intellectual conversion is largely a matter of getting beyond this simple-minded objectivism, a realisation that it is not by a journey outwards that we encounter reality but by a journey inwards, a realisation that the way to reality is through self-appropriation.

So it is that when we come to examine the method of theology, we must look not at the subject-matter of theology but at the mind of the theologian, seeing the data (revelation etc.) in terms of the cognitional structure of man as dynamically orientated towards God. But we would miss the whole point of the book if we saw it as purely descriptive and analytic. It is primarily a practical manual of self-appropriation for the theologian. Through it the theologian comes to know himself as a theologian, and so comes to know what theology is or should be. And since everything is based on the *invariant* structures of intentional consciousness the work is in its essentials definitive and final.

One can forgive Lonergan for falling victim to what may be called 'the philosopher's fallacy', the conviction that here at last is the whole truth and nothing but the truth. Nearly all the great philosophers have thought likewise; perhaps the illusion provides the necessary dynamism for living laborious days. The fact that one does not have to take this kind of claim seriously does not at all mean that we do not take the work of the philosopher seriously. And, since enough has been said already to indicate why I do not take Lonergan's claim seriously, I would like to conclude with one or two considerations (there are many others) which help to convince me of the importance of Lonergan's contribution to theological method.

Lonergan has shifted the whole debate on theological method from the operation to the operator, from the object to the subject. Instead of looking at the kind of work that theologians do, we are asked to look at the theologian at work, and to situate this work in relation to the basic structures of his personality. We are asked especially to pose the crucial question of the theologian's person-to-person relationship with the God he interprets. Lonergan's achievement in *Method in Theology* is to have placed in question the concept of a neutral, objectivist theology, whether understood statically or as conditioned by history. Theology becomes an *I-Thou* enterprise in which the *I* pole of the relationship is given full value. We are forced to see the Augustinian *noverim me, noverim te* as a principle not merely of spiritual growth but of theological method.

Those who have already accepted *Insight* as the definitive *summa* of philosophy will be ready to accept this shift from object to subject as revolutionary. Those who cannot do this may, nevertheless, find that it is necessary to take account of the subjective pole in their approach to theological method. The polar tension of subject and object is, or should be, creative at all levels of cognitive activity. Those who feel that philosophy has its starting point and centre of reference not in knowing but in reality as the object of our fundamental awareness, are led by Lonergan to examine the structures according to which this awareness develops and clarifies itself. Knowing and being are correlative, and the polar tension of subject and object is but a particular expression of the pull of the infinite on the finite.

Further, Lonergan's exploration of the subject for the benefit of theology may lead others to other kinds of exploration of the subject. There are, for instance, those apparently negative human dimensions which express the reciprocity of the finite and infinite, and which, because reciprocity in terms of love implies a kind of equality, are manifestations of specifically human greatness. If man is dynamism he is also response and receptivity, open to the invitation of the infinite, waiting on the infinite. The Lord is long in coming because man must discover the full dimensions of his waiting. Waiting, loneliness, 'nothingness', pathos: these are some of the seemingly negative human dimensions which are the necessary correlatives of the divine abundance. An infinity of giving looks to an infinity of receiving, and the receptive dimension can only unfold gradually, being constantly forced to relinquish what has been received so that a greater may be received.

These seemingly negative dimensions are as truly self-transcending as are the dynamisms of intentional consciousness, and their exploration involves an even more delicately and distinctively human self-appropriation. It is here especially that the theologian is in need of the help of the poet and the artist, for the theologian 'appropriates' himself as a theologian only if he also appropriates himself as a man.

> Look, beloved child, into my eyes, see there
> Yourself, mirrored in that living water
> From whose deep pools all images of earth are born.

The poet's voice, here a woman's voice also, reminds theological man of one of the essential dimensions of his being as a theologian. It is only through the appropriation in maturity, in terms of maturity, of the dimension of childhood that a man can speak meaningfully of God.

This, for me, indicates what is best in Bernard Lonergan's writing: a mystical receptivity; openness to far horizons; a curious innocence: the lover of God whose insights of the heart are mediated by (too much, perhaps) theological meaning.

NOTES

1 See E. A. Sillem, *George Berkeley and the Proofs for the Existence of God*, Longmans, Green, 1957, 166, 167.
2 *Encyclopedia of the Philosophical Sciences* 126.
3 *Method in Theology* 6.
4 *Ibid.* 240.

5   *Ibid*. 25.
6   *Insight* 354
7   *Ibid*.
8   *Ibid*. 348.
9   *Ibid*. 484.
10 For a subtle and penetrating critique of Lonergan's notion of being see Desmond Connell, 'Father Lonergan and the Idea of Being', *The Irish Theological Quarterly*, Vol. 37, n. 2 (April 1970). I do not think that Fr. Connell takes sufficient account of the main drift of *Insight* as 'an essay in aid of personal appropriation of one's own rational self-consciousness' (p. 743), and so, his conclusions are perhaps too negative; nevertheless Lonergan's assertions about being come rather badly out of Fr. Connell's analysis. Nor has anybody, as far as I know, attempted to meet Fr. Connell's criticisms.
11 *Insight* 355.
12 *Method in Theology* 22.
13 *Ibid*. 12.
14 *Ibid*. 10.
15 *Ibid*. 121.
16 *Ibid*.
17 *Ibid*. 122.
18 *Ibid*.
19 *Ibid*. 14.

A Note on Lonergan and a Greek Conception of Science

Gerard Watson

The second sentence of Lonergan's *Method in Theology* begins: 'The classicist notion of culture was normative: at least *de jure* there was but one culture that was both universal and permanent.' What was 'the classicist notion'? In this first paragraph it is illuminated only by being contrasted with 'the empirical notion of culture' which is 'the set of meanings and value that informs a way of life'. This distinction, so far not sufficiently clear, is fundamental to his book, because the next paragraph says: 'When the classicist notion of culture prevails, theology is conceived as a permanent achievement, and then one discourses on its nature. When culture is conceived empirically, theology is known to be an ongoing process, and then one writes on its method.'

The distinction between the two notions of culture is explained at some length later (p. 301). The classicist notion is one that has flourished for over two millenia. It stressed not facts but values. Its philosophy was the perennial philosophy. Classicist education was a matter of eternal verities and eternally valid laws. The classicist assumptions are those of stability, fixity and immutability. The natures of things are to be known adequately through the properties they possess and the laws they obey. Over and above the specific nature there is only individuation by matter so that the knowledge of one instance of a species is knowledge of any instance. Though Lonergan does not say so explicitly here it seems that he must be thinking of a Greek view. He speaks elsewhere (p. 6) of the distinctive operation of modern science and how it contrasts with the 'static fixity that results from Aristotle's concentration on the necessary and immutable'.

In *Collection* (pp. 259-260) Lonergan states clearly to whom he is referring:

> The Greek conception (of science) was formulated by Aristotle in his *Posterior Analytics*: it envisaged science as true, certain knowledge of causal necessity. But modern science is not true, it is only on the way towards truth. It is not certain; for its

55

positive affirmations it claims no more than probability. It is not knowledge but hypothesis, theory, system, the best available scientific opinion of the day. Its object is not necessity but verified possibility.[1]

Comment begins here. To speak of 'the Greek conception' implies that there was only one Greek conception and it is stated that Aristotle was responsible for it. It should be pointed out first of all that there are ambiguities in 'science' which are not apparent in this extract from Lonergan. The word that he is translating 'science' is (presumably) *epistēmē*. It might have been fairer to Aristotle to distinguish between a principle of scientific research and an ideal of the presentation of scientific truth (see Allan, *The Philosophy of Aristotle*, p. 122), to examine his concept of *Techne*, and in general to look at Aristotle's practical procedure in the various branches of knowledge in which he interested himself, reading especially his remarks in *De partibus animalium* on 'high' and 'low' science. He has harsh words to say on 'Those whom devotion to long discussions has rendered unobservant of fact, (and who) are too ready to dogmatize on the basis of a few observations' (*De generatione et corruptione*, 316a9).

But we can leave to one side the treatment of Aristotle to emphasise that Aristotle's conception of science, whatever we decide that it is, was not the only Greek conception of science. There was at least one other school which was also prominent for centuries and which provides a parallel to Lonergan's description of modern science which is, perhaps, uncomfortably close and for that reason unsuitable for Lonergan's theory. This was the Stoic school and it is interesting to compare what Lonergan says of modern science with some positions of theirs.

Lonergan says that modern science is not true but only on the way towards truth, not certain but probable, not knowledge but hypothesis. The Stoics also considered the problem of truth. They distinguished 'the true' and 'Truth' (SVF II 132). Truth is knowledge assertoric of all true propositions, an ordered system constructed from true propositions. But 'the true' is just one proposition. Men have to work with such single propositions. The perfect *logos* to which the world aspires would imply perfect awareness but we have not reached this perfection. We are aware of only one separate particular at each separate moment and we ourselves are a different 'thing' at each moment. How then are we to achieve a coherent knowledge of the universe?

The Stoics maintained that relations and divisions between events are imposed by our minds and expressed in propositions. Language permits a much wider range of reality: a wider selection of sequences is at his disposal for inspection, abstraction and comparison, thus allowing more analysis of causality. So man can predict courses of events and state the law of certain types of events. The concordance of gradually verified predictions establishes the coherence of perfect knowledge or *logos*.

The examples given in Stoic logic are all of singular propositions: they make no room for the Aristotelian universal proposition. The importance of the conditional is very obvious in Stoic propositional logic. They seem to consider that such a proposition is a better reflection of our knowledge of the universe. The knowledge is fragmented yet can be gradually brought towards completion.

The Stoics take great care with the language employed to express causality. In order to give a proper description of causation it would be necessary to know everything: reality for them is a dynamic continuum, as Sambursky has expressed it. We are forced to make a selection from the preconditions we can arrive at and presume that some of these are the most important. Strictly speaking our statement should bring out the fact that in our ordinary language we are normally imposing a pattern. So we should say 'A is the cause to B of a predicate', thus separating what is our contribution, the interpretation we are putting on events. Through this language, by hypothetical enunciations, one approaches a reliable law of events. Absolute certainty is not always possible in particular cases. Our guide through life is the reasonable proposition, the *eulogon*, one with more chances of being true than not.

So there are chances of reconciliation between Lonergan's modern ideal and *a* Greek conception. What influence had Stoic philosophy? I think it will be agreed without argument that it was very great, even within the Church itself (cf. Spanneut's *Le Stoicisme des Pères de l'Eglise*). Why then was their method not adopted by the Church in the development of its theology? To attempt to answer that question would take me far beyond my brief which was merely to raise a question about the notion of a monolithic classicist culture. An indication of some of the questions that could be asked might lead to a change of emphasis in Lonergan. Was it some intellectual poverty in the early Church which blinded it to the merits of the Stoic approach and forced her to choose Platonist-Aristotelianism in its place? Or was it some other reason such as the attraction of the Platonist-Aristotelian ideal of total knowledge, an ideal which seemed to conform better to the high estimate of a theology which was after all taken to contain the perfect revelation? A tentative cast of mind might seem unworthy of God's certain truth. It is interesting, for instance, to see that the Church did not accept Aristotle's reservations about exactness in ethics, whatever about the influence of classicist culture on theology. Is it not the perennial danger for theology, to mistake aspiration, total understanding, for achievement? Some of the large claims made in Lonergan's own work make one wonder if he has wholly escaped the infection himself.

Perhaps there is a different question here at issue than the one which Lonergan raises. It is not so much the conception of culture at any period that determines the way of doing theology, but the Church's understanding of itself that determines which method shall be favoured from among those which the culture offers. The Church was well aware of the Greek scientific outlook. There is no easy answer as to why she turned away from it. What would Lonergan say of John Philoponos whom Sambursky (*The Physical World of Late Antiquity*, p. 150) calls 'the last great thinker of antiquity . . . whose original ideas restored scientific thought to its classical heights' but who also shows the deteriorating effect that a conformist attitude to the Church had on the spirit of scientific inquiry? This is to be seen in the contrast between his earlier works and the *De Opificio Mundi*. In this latter work he says that one should not inquire into the last causes nor ask too many questions. 'Only this we all believe — that God had created everything beautifully and as it was needed, neither more nor less. Altogether we know the causes of only a few things, and if people cannot tell the natural causes of the manifest things, they should not ask us about the causes of the hidden ones.' (III 4 (116, 22)).

NOTE

1 I owe this reference and much other information about Lonergan to Paul Surlis. See his 'Rahner and Lonergan on Method in Theology', II. *I.T.Q.* 39 (1972), 23-42.

Lonergan and Method in the Natural Sciences

Mary Hesse

In his approach to natural science, Lonergan's *Insight* might be called an induction from the methods of science to those of knowledge and understanding in general, while his *Method*[1] follows from the start the hypothetical method of delineating a scheme for all of knowledge, within which natural science has a definite though subordinate rôle. This progression from 1957 to 1972 is in line with the earlier trend from inductivism to hypothetico-deductivism in the philosophy of natural science itself, and it promises corresponding progress in its approach to problems of method in theology. However, Lonergan is not the first methodologist to fall victim to the 'cultural lag' between philosophy of science and philosophy of religion. Just at the point when philosophers of science are rejecting hypothetico-deductivism and raising fundamentally new and sceptical questions about the relation of natural science to the phenomena of cultural change and cross-cultural meanings, Lonergan not only presents a science which is as stable and self-confident within its own domain as any nineteenth-century mechanist could desire, but also bases his whole model of method upon the very assumptions of progressive accumulation, and of the differentiation of knowledge into relatively independent 'specialties' that are currently under attack. In what follows I shall try to justify these comments by showing:

(1) That the continuities Lonergan finds within his general schema of knowledge, of which natural science is a part, still owe too much to a questionable cumulative model of natural science;

(2) That his philosophy of science is uncritical, and fails to make use of the illumination which current debates could throw upon his own more general problems, particularly those concerning the relation between the natural and the human sciences; and

(3) That he fails to make out the claim to objectivity of the so-called 'levels of consciousness' which go beyond natural science, and to which he principally assigns the human sciences and theology.

THE METHOD OF NATURAL SCIENCE

In *Insight* mathematics and science are explicitly made the model of a certain kind of 'insight', and are intended to introduce the reader to that concept in a relatively clear and amenable type of application. This aim is prosecuted through several chapters in which increasingly complex scientific theories are discussed, ranging from geometry through classical and quantum physics to Darwinian evolution. Throughout, general morals are drawn, not only with regard to the nature of 'insight', but to more technical concepts such as causality, necessity, probability, complementarity, and emergent evolution. This is not the place to comment on the details of these discussions, since *Method* is not concerned directly with such substantive concepts of either science or theology. Indeed, the first chapter of *Method* contains what may almost be taken as a repudiation of a framework in which science has such a central place: we are told that the method of science has for too long been assumed to be the only successful method, and that method in theology is not here to be discussed on its analogy. Science is rather to be seen as having its primary place in the first and second levels of a four-level hierarchy of human consciousness or intentionality: the empirical or commonsense; the intellectual or theoretical; the rational, or interior judging of facts; and the responsible, or deciding on values. The catch-words relating to this four-fold categorial framework are pervasive throughout the book: experiencing, understanding, judging, deciding, or 'Be attentive, Be intelligent, Be reasonable, Be responsible' (9, 20). These are held to be present as transcendental presuppositions in every domain of knowledge from commonsense through science and history to theology, but while the intrinsic goals of science terminate at the second level, and those of history at the third level, theology is concerned with all four levels and most specifically with the fourth.

Many questions arise about this classification, and I cannot be confident that the apparently neat summary just given has correctly captured Lonergan's intentions. In particular, there are many places where theoretical science seems to be definitely assigned to the second level (e.g. 212-3), and to provide theoretical correction for commonsense beliefs in terms of scientific theories, as in the explanatory framework of modern physics (84-85). At the same time, however, there are other places where the operations at the second level seem remote from theoretical science. For example, in the chapter in which Lonergan is explicitly considering the second level of understanding in theology, with its corresponding 'functional specialty' of 'Interpretation', he is concerned mainly with the *hermeneutic* model of interpretation of texts, as typically in historical study. Euclidean geometry, which is taken in *Insight* to be a paradigm of mathematical science, is here said not to require 'interpretation' (153), and yet later (213) it is said to depend on a ground of 'insight', and seems to be an example of the second level. Again, later, science is said to largely escape the hermeneutic circle in which interpretative history is caught (248), and yet this circle arises first at the second level. The appearance of logical rigour in Lonergan's classification here, as too often in the book, reveals ambiguity and even superficiality in face of a little logical probing.

However that may be, the scheme of *Method* is profoundly anti-reductionist, and constitutes an attempt to develop a comparative epistemology of different domains of knowledge. The first questions that must be asked about it relate to the accuracy of the implied description of natural science, and to the distinctions implied between the natural and the human sciences, particularly history. These are questions which have been much canvassed in 'secular' literature, and will therefore constitute a test of the soundness of Lonergan's philosophical method relative to current debate, preparatory to the task (which is fortunately not my task here) of evaluating his discussions of the much more problematic and much less well understood area of method in theology.

Early in the first chapter of *Method*, Lonergan gives a succinct description of method in the natural sciences, which both expresses his implicit philosophy of science, and is also meant to serve as a model for the second level of method in general, as far as it is shared by all the sciences including theology:

> ... the process of experimentation yields new data, new observations, new descriptions that may or may not confirm the hypothesis that is being tested. ... The wheel of method not only turns but also rolls along. The field of observed data keeps broadening. New discoveries and theories express not only the new insights but also all that was valid in the old, to give method its cumulative character and to engender the conviction that, however remote may still be the goal of the complete explanation of all phenomena, at least we now are nearer to it than we were. (5)

This summary, he goes on, 'illustrates a preliminary notion of method as *a normative pattern of recurrent and related operation yielding cumulative and progressive results.*' (5, his italics). What natural science is assumed to share with all cognitive enterprises, then, are certain characteristics of method: it is dynamic, recursive, self-corrective, and progresses by accumulating truth to an ideal goal of complete and univocal explanation.

Lonergan is indeed wise to restrict the aspects of science that can serve as a model for knowledge, to method rather than substantive results. He rightly sees that the natural sciences can no longer be claimed to have attained any final or necessary truth. But his reliance on a limited set of authorities for scientific method leads him to neglect the epistemological *problem* that is posed by this abandonment of the claim that 'science shows that' for the weaker programme of 'better and better approximations to an ideal truth'. In fact recent developments in philosophy of science strongly suggest that this weaker programme was only an unstable resting point between classical nineteenth-century confidence and late twentieth-century scepticism and relativism. For the difficulty in determining what constitutes nearer and nearer approach to the truth through a sequence of scientific revolutions has led to radical questioning of the notion of the goal of 'complete explanation' which is here made a presupposition of method. The work of Kuhn, Feyerabend,[2] and others, has shown that theoretical science proceeds by postulating sequences of conceptually quite different models of the world — from discrete atoms to continuous fields to quantized fields; from the continuous scale of being to catastrophic discontinuities to natural selection by mutation; from Euclidean space and time to Minkowskian space-time to non-simply connected topologies of space-time; and so on. The very dynamic character of the method of science itself makes it highly likely that indefinitely many conceptual switches as radical as these will occur in the future if science itself survives, and makes it highly problematic to maintain that science is approaching nearer and nearer to any sort of unique and total understanding of the natural world. Moreover, far from seeing theoretical science as autonomous with respect to other disciplines, as Lonergan suggests it is (94), historical and philosophical studies of science indicate the strong reciprocal influences at work between the theoretical models adopted in science and the conceptual frameworks of metaphysics and theology, and more recently, of studies of society and of history.

That Lonergan adopts this questionable cumulative model of natural science might be unimportant, were it not that in this respect at least he wishes to say that the method of science is typical of all method. This means that the movements in history and philosophy of science I have just sketched must be unpalatable to him in two sorts of respect. The first is his implicit tendency, despite an occasional explicit realism with regard to theoretical science (259), to interpret science as essentially instrumental. Science, he holds, is concerned not with causes but only with probable correlations, not with things but with increasing understanding of sensible data (94, 293, 315). Data, moreover, are to be distinguished from 'facts', which are the product of third-level judgment upon data, as in historical studies that are oriented towards the human meanings of events (202, 348). These instrumentalist tendencies are indeed most clearly seen in the distinctions drawn by Lonergan between the characteristics of the natural and the human sciences and theology, which I consider in the next section.

Now there is no doubt that, viewed instrumentally and technologically, there is progressive accumulation of a sort in natural science. But it is not clear that this sort of progress does all that Lonergan wants of a model of method. As we have seen, it does not in itself entail the progression of *theoretical* science towards total and unique explanations, as Lonergan's own descriptions of its self-corrective and hypothetical method ought to have shown him. Without progress on this second level of theoretical understanding there seems little basis for relying on the progress of merely instrumental science as a cognitive model for other disciplines. And yet the reconstruction of 'facts' from data which is required at the third level in history and theology is explicitly said to depend on the results of theoretical investigation at the second level (202). What form of progress is left to either of these disciplines if they, like science, are inevitably based on theoretical reconstructions which depend heavily on viewpoint, and are circularly reinforced by the very historiographical and theological conclusions they are supposed to support? Lonergan cannot convincingly use natural science as his methodological model of progress here without taking account of the philosophical controversies that now surround this concept, and in particular without noting that the prestige afforded by the apparently cumulative character of science in the nineteenth century has by now worn more than a little thin.

The second reason why debates about progress and relativity in theoretical science are of central and destructive importance to Lonergan's thesis is that he takes progress in other cognitive disciplines very seriously, apparently for no better reason than that progress is held to be exhibited in natural science and has therefore become constitutive of method in general. The importance of this postulate of progression to unique truth is seen most clearly in the really astonishing claims made for the goals of both history and theology. With regard to history, Lonergan seems to see 'perspectivism' as a merely accidental result of the historian's own contingent immersion in the historical process. But

> Were [the historian's] information complete, his understanding all-comprehensive, his every judgment certain, then there would be room neither for selection nor for perspectivism. Then historical reality would be known in its fixity and its unequivocal structures. (218)

A few pages later it is made clear that access to 'complete data' would not in itself ensure that the objective reality of history is realized: the empiricist is mistaken in thinking that 'objectivity is a matter of seeing all that's there to be seen and seeing nothing that's not there' (232). Objectivity both in history and theology is ensured only the intellectual 'conversion' of the investigator: in regard to theology

> the real menace to unity of faith does not lie either in the many brands of common sense or the many differentiations of human consciousness. It lies in the absence of intellectual or moral or religious conversion (330).

I shall return to these claims for 'intellectual conversion' presently; meanwhile in questioning the assumption of such univocal goals of historical and theological studies I need not add to the perceptive comments of Father Lash on this topic in the first section of his paper in this volume.

DIFFERENTIAE OF THE NATURAL AND HUMAN SCIENCES

Lonergan makes many of the by-now familiar distinctions between the methods and subject-matters of the natural and human sciences, following the non-positivist traditions of Vico, Dilthey and Collingwood. In these traditions the principal distinction is held to be that the objects of natural science are not constituted by acts of *meaning* (179), while in the human sciences meaning is all pervasive. This distinction has always been found peculiarly elusive in positivist and analytic circles, and it is therefore important to see whether Lonergan's account of it throws much light on the difficulties.

It is a truism that natural science, like geography, is about things like maps, whereas history is about chaps. But it is not so easy to determine what is the precise significance of the remark that the world of human meaning (actions, intentions, cultures, symbolism, language) form part of the subject-matter of the human and not of the natural sciences. What significance has it for the methods, aims, and results of these sciences? Cannot the complex structures of human society be investigated 'from the outside' in the same way as the complex structures of atoms or galaxies? In the Dilthean tradition Lonergan says No: to investigate social science, psychology or history externally is to eliminate meaning and consciousness. In these sciences the investigator himself, as conscious human being, is of the same kind as his subject-matter, and sometimes, as in contemporary sociology and politics, actually a part of what he is studying. Several consequences are held to flow from this.

First there is the implied claim of 'privileged access'. The doings of human individuals and societies are held to be rehearsable in in the investigator's mind in a manner not open to him when examining the doings of atoms and galaxies. The appropriate mode of explanation in historical science is therefore said to be narrative, and the understanding of particulars in commonsense categories involving 'insight', as opposed to the universal, technically expressed, law-like systems of natural science, in which there is continuous external testing by intersubjectively acceptable data. Unlike many writers in this vein, Lonergan does not underestimate the element of theoretical interpretation or understanding in natural science — there is 'meaning' in scientific theories, and it is meaning which can on occasion challenge the meanings of commonsense, as in the example of Eddington's two tables to which Lonergan frequently reverts. But this 'meaning' is at the second level of his four-fold hierarchy, and human meaning on the other hand involves the third level of 'interior judgment'.

That a distinction is made between these two levels, however, seems to depend entirely on the claim of privileged access by introspection to the thoughts and intentions of men. But it is by no means clear that there is any such privileged access. One need only be reminded of Wittgenstein's arguments against 'private languages'. Independently of these arguments there are also the facts about the thought-forms of distant cultures, which are brought increasingly to light by modern anthropology, where it is far from obvious that introspection of our own thought-forms is much help, or is even relevant, to the understanding of the foreign culture. Just as theoretical science depends on imaginative reconstruction of systematic interpretations of data with the aid of models and metaphors, so understanding of much human behaviour and belief depends on reconstruction from external clues, using whatever models come usefully to hand. These may sometimes be models from non-human nature, as in evolutionary theories of human society, and sometimes models from man. (Models from man may also be used in natural science, for example the telephone-exchange model of the brain.) No case has been conclusively made out by Lonergan from the privileged access argument for his second and third level distinction.

Secondly, the human sciences are said to be inevitably caught in the so-called 'hermeneutic circle'. Data are understood only in terms of interpretation and of the interior judgment of the investigator, whose own social and historical perspective colours the interpretation. Thus, data are used to reconstruct facts in the light of particular human viewpoints, and objective knowledge is in danger of degenerating into a plurality of self-reinforcing subjective myths. Lonergan holds that natural science largely escapes this circle, because of its amenability to testing by independent and intersubjective empirical data. He does, however, qualify this conclusion by reference to a currently popular example among Continental phenomenologists: Bohr's doctrine of complementarity in quantum mechanics, in which the possibility of a sharp separation between knowing subject and known object even in physics is rejected (248). This example is, of course, highly controversial in physics, but Lonergan gives no hint of these controversies here, and the single authority he cites is not generally representative.[3] The example is a bad one if it is used as a general argument for an irreducible interference produced by the investigator upon the objects of his study, because many situations are well known in physics in which the understanding of relevant law-like relations is so complete that the effects of the investigator's interference can also be calculated in advance (we can easily correct for the slight cooling produced by introducing a thermometer into a hot bath, and calculate the original temperature of the bath). The special characteristic of current quantum physics is that it itself contains a postulate (the uncertainty principle) that forbids such corrective calculations on pain of inconsistency. But current quantum physics has not been *proved* to be true, any more than any other part of theoretical science; hence this postulate may possibly be dropped in the future. Arguments for the irreducible interference of subject and object in knowledge must be based on grounds different from those of physics alone, and Lonergan does not produce any. Nothing that has yet been said in the Dilthean tradition has conclusively shown that laws of human behaviour exactly analogous to the laws of theoretical science are in principle impossible, nor that they would necessarily be incomplete.[4]

However, by introducing philosophical show-pieces of modern science such as Eddington's tables and Bohr's complementarity, Lonergan does have one laudable motive. He intends to show that the distinctions between natural and human sciences marked by the second and third realm of meaning are not absolute. He envisages rather a continuum of aspects of all sciences, requiring all levels of understanding to some degree. Even the fourth level of transcendent moral decision, where theology is principally at home, is also said to be relevant to natural science, through the involvement of science in technological and social policies (248, 317). Once the distinctions are blurred in this way, however, it is difficult to see what they amounted to in the first place.

Thirdly, the human sciences are frequently held to involve irreducible questions of value with which the natural sciences are unconcerned. Lonergan does not entirely accept this characterization of the natural sciences as we have just seen; however, for him social value contexts are marginal to natural science, and he also believes that they are not the proper concern even of historical science. Here he adopts something like Max Weber's distinction between social science and social policy: 'history . . . is not directly concerned to promote social and cultural goals . . . [which] can exercise not only a disturbing but even a distorting influence on historical investigation' (232). The historian may, indeed, make value-judgments in selecting those things that are worth knowing, but in doing this he is acting outside his 'specialty', which is solely aimed at 'settling matters of fact by appealing to empirical evidence'.

Again, in proposing these views, Lonergan relies on selected authorities and gives no hint that these questions have been subject to radical and continuous debate in the literature of analytical philosophy of science for several decades. Rehearsal of the Weberian distinction, without serious supporting arguments and examples, does scant justice to the increasing awareness among sociologists that some of their theoretical conflicts are ideological in nature, that is to say, that they import value judgments into the very experiencing of data and their interpretation.[5] There is, indeed, currently a tendency towards ideological relativism in the human sciences just as there is with regard to the theories of natural science. It is these tendencies, to which Lonergan seems all but oblivious, that pose the greatest threat to the concept of objective method.

OBJECTIVITY

The question of objectivity is indeed the most important problem that arises from Lonergan's elaboration of his four levels of meaning, and the assignment of different specialities principally to one or other of them. The distinction between the second level of theoretical understanding and the third level of interior judgment is not clearly made out, as I have argued, but at least it is helpful in permitting Lonergan to avoid the a-theoretical instrumentalization of natural science that frequently accompanies comparative analyses of method. I have already noted that, except for his uncritical belief in the cumulative character of scientific truth, Lonergan is perceptive in his description of the dynamic, self-corrective method of natural science, and its reciprocal interactions with the first, or commonsense, level of meaning. He relies here upon the now classic phase of philosophy of science, perhaps best represented by Nagel's authoritative text of 1961,[6] in which a highly sophisticated account of the method of natural science is elaborated, and shown to be fit to stand beside earlier empiricist epistemologies as a paradigm of objective knowledge. Now, however, as Lonergan shows himself well aware in the first pages of his book, the problem is that there is no such generally acceptable paradigm for the objective character of historical science, let alone theology, and this problem is compounded just in so far as the recent historicist developments in philosophy of science I have described are taken to supercede Nagel's model even in the natural sciences. The final judgment of *Method* must rest upon the answer to the question whether Lonergan here provides, at least in outline, new and adequate paradigms of objective knowledge.

One cannot confidently give an affirmative answer. Lonergan is not unaware that the basic problem is one of psychologism or *subjectivism*. Indeed, he clearly regards his schema of knowledge as in a sense an advance from the metaphysical to the psychological, particularly in relation to theology:

> ... the basic terms and relations of systematic theology will be not metaphysical, as in medieval theology, but psychological. ... For every term and relation there still exists a corresponding element in intentional consciousness. Accordingly, empty or misleading terms and relations can be eliminated, while valid ones can be elucidated by the conscious intention from which they are derived. The importance of such a critical control will be evident to anyone familiar with the vast arid wastes of theological controversy. (343)

A primary concern of the epistemology of the sciences, however, has been to go beyond psychology to objectivity, or at least to intersubjectivity. Lonergan claims that in recent philosophy there has been an unjustified shift in the meanings of the terms objective and subjective. Objective knowledge is now that upon which general agreement is possible, as in mathematics and science; whereas in philosophy, ethics and religion, where agreement is generally lacking, only subjective results can be obtained. But this, he claims, is to neglect the further question of the truth or value of such subjectivity, and he rightly points out that the answer to this question is not entailed by the criterion of general agreement. He therefore argues that objectivity cannot be equated with the naïve realism that accepts the real as mediated only by commonsense or by theoretical reason, and depends on no further injection of human meaning. It must be regarded rather as the fruit of the *right* interpretations on the third and fourth levels:

> . . . it is now apparent that in the world mediated by meaning and motivated by value, objectivity is simply the consequence of authentic subjectivity, of genuine attention, genuine intelligence, genuine reasonableness, genuine responsibility. (265)

So far, however, this analysis does not contribute much to the question whether detailed criteria can be given for this kind of objectivity. To this question Lonergan has two types of response. The first lies in a 'critical realism' which posits the ideal goal of total and univocal truth for the human sciences and theology as well as for natural science. The second lies in his reliance upon the interior state of the investigator as the guarantor of objectivity. I have already pointed out some objections to the first posit. As for the second, although there is pervasive reference in *Method* to the *truth* of the intellectual and value judgments that emanate from the 'authentic subjectivity' of the 'converted' individual, there is no discussion of the question how we are to recognize such authenticity or conversion, short of the circular method of subjecting ourselves to the same intellectual and religious discipline that Lonergan recommends. But how is *this* to be distinguished with regard to truth and objectivity from the psychic conditioning of any other religious asceticism, or of secularism, or indeed of some form of devil-worship? Lonergan will doubtless reply by repeating 'Be attentive, Be intelligent, Be reasonable, Be responsible', in the transcendent faith that these injunctions will lead us into the unique and authentic circle.[7] But Christendom has been too full of sects of warring theologians and philosophers (warring in fact as well as in words) to allow us to suppose that following Lonergan's injunctions will dispense us from hard and testing attempts at philosophical argument and the rational elaboration of non-psychological criteria of objectivity. And this need is only reinforced by the reflection that outside Christendom, perhaps particularly today, there have been many Cyruses of the intellect from whom the Church does well to learn.

There is finally a matter more intimately connected with Lonergan's philosophical style that precludes *Method* from being a valuable contribution to the current philosophical debate. This is a certain detachment from interior philosophical wrestling which one senses in his discourse, and a certain absence of first-hand engagement with the methodological problems of the natural sciences and of history.[8] I have already remarked on the absence of detailed philosophical argument and careful analysis of examples in his text, and his reliance upon selected authorities. It is true that a similar didactic style is common to most Continental philosophy and to much theology both Anglo-Saxon and Continental. It may even be held that the desire for excessively nit-picking logical analyses is a peculiar fashion of recent Anglo-Saxon philosophy and should be discarded as unprofitable. But no one versed in the Western philosophical tradition, as Lonergan clearly is, can possibly question the value of genuine hard-hitting philosophical argument. It is more likely that Lonergan's own final reliance on 'insight', 'conversion', and the 'love of God' has persuaded him that once through the needle-eye of conversion, philosophical agonizing is superseded, since all problems have by now fallen into place in the total schema of knowledge. If this were indeed the explanation of his style, it would surely betray great insensitivity to the powerful rational arguments which have been mounted on behalf of reductionism, secularism, and even forms of theism other than that espoused by Lonergan himself.[9] Even at the level of 'communications' with his fellow English-speaking philosophers, it would have been wiser to have adopted a greater measure of their style, and to have entered with greater involvement into their problems.

NOTES

1 B. J. F. Lonergan, *Insight, a Study of Human Understanding*, London, 1957; *Method in Theology*, London, 1972. References in brackets in the text will be to page numbers of *Method*.
2 Particularly T. S. Kuhn, *The Structure of Scientific Revolutions*, second ed. Chicago, 1970; and P. K. Feyerabend, 'Explanation, reduction and empiricism', *Minnesota Studies in the Philosophy of Science*, III, ed. H. Feigl and G. Maxwell, Minneapolis, 1962, p. 28, and many other papers by Feyerabend.
3 In *Insight* there is a confusing assimilation of the notion of 'complementarity' to the relation between 'classical and statistical procedures' (Chap. IV). This is not how the notion is generally understood in physics, where it refers either to the complementarity of the two *classical* models of wave and particles, or (in Bohr, and this interpretation is not generally acceptable among physicists) to the irreducible multiplicity of viewpoints allegedly generated by the need to separate subject and object in knowledge. For the illuminating suggestion that Bohr's

views are derived rather from Kierkkegaardian philosophy and Jamesian psychology than from physics itself, see M. Jammer, *The Conceptual Development of Quantum Mechanics*, New York, 1966, pp. 166 f., 349 f.

4 I do not wish to be taken to be denying here that there *may be* such arguments, only that they are not to be found in the Dilthean tradition. See my 'In defence of objectivity', *Proceedings of the British Academy*, 1972.

5 For a careful and sympathetic examination of this question within an analytic framework, see C. Taylor, 'Interpretation and the sciences of man', *Rev. Met.*, 25, 1971.

6 E. Nagel, *The Structure of Science*, New York, 1961.

7 Even Barth and Bultmann have not arrived: 'In both Barth and Bultmann . . . there is revealed the need for intellectual as well as moral and religious conversion' (318)!

8 It is ominous that he considers that while the theologian *carries out the* the functional specialties, 'The methodologist has *the far lighter task* of indicating what the various tasks of theologians are and how each presupposes or complements the others' (355, my italics). Have all the recent discussions about the cognitive status of theology and the meaning of its linguistic expressions then been carried on in vain? But Lonergan is clearly not troubled by such questions: for example, after paraphrasing the notorious declaration of Athanasius on consubstantiality, he can say: 'Now the meaning of this declaration is luminous'—only to a *logically trained mind* does it raise a question . . .(277)!

9 Cf. the startlingly abrupt dismissal of the atheist's or humanist's rejection of the 'transcendental tendency of the human spirit that . . . comes to the question of God': 'But their negations *presuppose* the spark in our clod, our native orientation to the divine' (103). One might as validly argue from the natural human interest in the future to a deep significance of the 'question of astrology'.

Theological Disagreement and the Functional Specialties

Elizabeth Maclaren

THE PROBLEM

Method in Theology is so intricately argued that pulling out any one strand tends to unravel the entire fabric of the text. It is hardly possible, therefore, to explore or criticise his account of theological disagreement without reference to the whole framework of the book. Nevertheless, the focus of this essay is the single question whether Lonergan's description of the theological enterprise in terms of functional specialties does justice to the problem of theological disagreement.

What *is* the problem? Lonergan rarely raises it explicitly, and when he does it is with a fairly soothing confidence that the answer is available:

> Christian theologians disagree not only on the areas relevant to theological research, but also on the interpretation of texts, on the occurrence of events, on the significance of movements. Such differences can have quite different grounds. Some may be eliminated by further progress in research, interpretation, history; and they can be left to the healing office of time. Some may result from developmental pluralism: there exist disparate cultures and diverse differentiations of consciousness; and such differences are to be bridged by working out the suitable transposition from one culture to another or from one differentiation of consciousness from another. Others, finally, arise because intellectual or moral or religious conversion has not occurred, and our chapters on *Dialectic* and the *Foundations* will attempt to indicate how these differences can be brought out into the open so that men of good will can discover one another. (p. 150-151)

The justification of such extended quotation is that it is a comprehensive *précis* of Lonergan's position on the matter. The rest if mere elaboration. It looks, therefore, as if the 'problem' of theological disagreement has virtually ceased to exist:

> My answer ... is to let Christian theologians begin from where they already stand. Each will consider one or more areas relevant to theological research. Let him work there. He will find that the method is designed to take care of the matter.
> *(Ibid.)*

In response to such bland optimism this paper will contend that the method may not so adequately take care of the matter.

LONERGAN'S FRAMEWORK

As preliminary to such a venture, the framework within which Lonergan sets the 'functional specialties' will stand repetition, if only to present concisely the relationships between 'background' and 'foreground'.

The four transcendental precepts have four corresponding levels of intentional operations, viz. experiencing, understanding, judgment, decision. Each of these levels recurs in two phases: (i) *oratio obliqua* and (ii) *oratio recta*. Given this, Lonergan offers a scheme of functional specialisation in theology which has some *prima facie* plausibility.

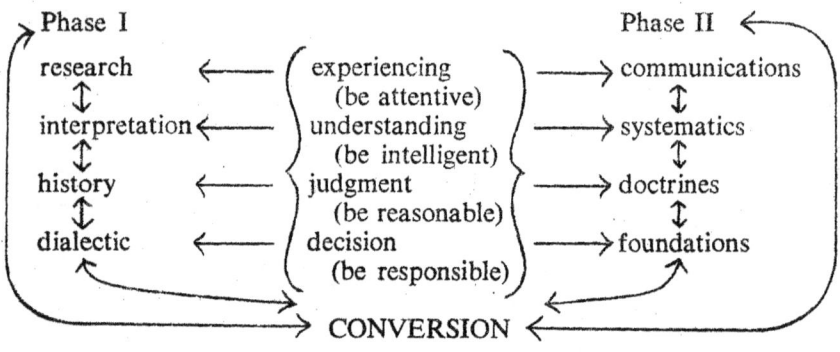

All the transcendental precepts are linked, and are involved in any single specialty, though each relates *primarily* to the one level as indicated in the diagram. There is possibility of mutual interaction among the eight, though Lonergan writes more often as if the direction of the interdependence was one way only, building up from research to the increasingly complex specialties.

Between Phase I and Phase II there is a basic shift which must be considered later, but which for the moment may simply be registered as 'conversion'. The matter is complicated, however, by the fact that even when conversion has taken place, its manifestations may vary enormously according to the differentiation of consciousness in the subject. The variations emerging from the realm of common sense, theory, interiority, religion and art afford thirty-one specific forms of converted consciousness (p. 271-272).

THEOLOGICAL DISAGREEMENT

It is now possible to see the outline of Lonergan's account of theological disagreement. Firstly, a theologian may fail to observe one or more of the transcendental precepts. Secondly, he may superficially disagree with others because of the manifold possibilities of expression resulting from variable differentiations of consciousness. Thirdly, and more malignantly, basic divergences are grounded 'in the heart of man' (p. 141), where the presence or absence of conversion so modifies horizons that radically different worlds are experienced.

Failure on one of these levels may affect all the functional specialties. In addition, specialists may apparently fail *within* their own field to 'produce the type of evidence proper to the specialty'. When each functions adequately,

> the exegete does exegesis on exegetical principles. The historian does history on historical principles. The doctrinal theologian ascertains doctrine on doctrinal principles. The systematic theologian clarifies, reconciles, unifies on systematic principles. (p. 137).

If this contention is to avoid the stigma of uninformative tautology, Lonergan's 'Foreground' has to provide identifying criteria for exegetical, historical, doctrinal, systematic principles. It is, however, doubtful whether the second half of the book actually succeeds in doing this. The dubiety crystallises round two points: one, the alleged correlation of specialties to levels of intentional operation, the other the relation between specialties and conversion.

The language used to describe the interrelation of specialties is curiously parallel to classical accounts of the interrelation of the Persons of the Trinity in relation to the world. As regards '*opera ad extra*' they are '*indivisa*', and yet the various works of salvation are said to belong '*terminative*' to one Person rather than another. Lonergan analogously insists (p. 133 H) that no theological operation can be done without obeying all the transcendental precepts, and yet that

> functional specializations arise inasmuch as one operates on all four levels to achieve the end proper to some particular level.

In Trinitarian discourse, the problem is that the doctrine of indivisibility of labour forecloses the possibility of identifying the Persons by what they do in the world. The subsequent ascription of what might be called functional specialties to Father, Son and Spirit then has an inevitable arbitrariness about it. Similarly, when Lonergan aims to relate concrete operations to one level rather than another, the impression is of capricious schematisation. In what sense is it more plausible to see History as operating on the level of judgment rather than of understanding, or Interpretation as understanding rather than judgment? Again, with Doctrines and Systematics, the levels might as plausibly be reversed; Dialectic seems as much a matter of judgment and understanding as of decision, while Communications is arguably more involved with decision than with experiencing.

The more one indulges in this exercise, the greater the air of haphazardness about it. This generates the suspicion, not that Lonergan has placed the specialties on the wrong levels, but that the 'levels' themselves are dubious. Indeed, the further one probes, the more blurred the differentiation of levels becomes. If experiencing is more than mere passive affectedness, if judgment involves any kind of selection, if understanding one's experience depends on judgments about it, then the 'levels' lose all plausibly distinct identity. Of course there are situations where one might choose one description rather than another, but the convincingness of this tends to be in inverse proportion to the complexity of the situation. If one holds that Beethoven is a greater musician that Brahms, or that apartheid is wrong, or that God's love implies universalism rather than the ultimate damnation of some, is one experiencing, understanding, judging or deciding? The difficulty about answering is not just a practical one of complexity of operation. It is a conceptual one, indicating that there are category mistakes afoot in the suggestion that each of these words corresponds to a distinct operation which excludes the others.

To argue in detail for the truth of this contention would take another essay. Its relevance to this one is as follows. If it is not true that specific levels appropriate to each specialty exist, any suggestion that theological disagreement arises from people operating on distinct levels is undermined. If an exegete and a doctrinal theologian disagree, this cannot be because they agree on one level (that of understanding) but disagree on a higher level (that of judgment). It is because they experience-understand-judge-decide differently.

To do Lonergan justice, one must say that in his foreground description of the functional specialties this complexity emerges. The trouble is that it puts such a strain on his formal schematization that the latter virtually disintegrates.

CONVERSION

A similar difficulty arises about the phasing of the specialties in relation to conversion. The first account of the distinction between Phase I and Phase II is in terms of theology 'in oratione obliqua' and 'in oratione recta'. Phase I involves telling what others have said about God in the past: Phase II is the theological confrontation with contemporary problems. At first glance, then, it looks as if the first four specialties are a matter of mere reporting, equally open to all investigators. Lonergan seems to say as much:

> However, in this earlier phase conversion is not a prerequisite; anyone can do research, interpret, write history, line up opposed positions. (p. 268)

Under further scrutiny, however, the demarcation line between the phases again blurs. The details of exegetical method involve the exegete in understanding the author and himself.

> But one's interpretation of others is affected by one's understanding of oneself, and the converted have a self to understand that is quite different from the self that the unconverted have to understand. (p. 271)

Similarly in Dialectic, the possibility of identifying positions and counter-positions correctly depends on having the *correct* foundational stance, and is therefore not neutrally open.

It is extraordinarily difficult to exegete Lonergan's mind on this issue without concluding that he is trying to have his uncommitment cake and to eat it. The relevance of self-understanding, the importance of human authenticity to every theological (as to every human) operation is documented in the foreground chapters. This makes sense of such utterances as,

> There is, perhaps inevitably, a dependence of the first phase on the second. (p. 143)

or

> Such conversion is operative, not only in the functional specialty, foundations, but also in the phase of mediating theology, in research, interpretation, history and dialectic. (p. 268)

or

> Conversion, as lived, affects all of a man's conscious and intentional operations. It directs his gaze, pervades his imagination, releases the symbols that penetrate to the depths of his psyche. It enriches his understanding, guides his judgments, reinforces his decisions.

What it does not make sense of are the qualifications, which appear to take with one hand what was given by the other:

> But the greatest care must be taken that this influence from the second phase does not destroy either the proper openness of the first phase to all relevant data or its proper function of reaching its results by an appeal to the data. (p. 143)

or

> When conversion is present and operative, [in the mediating phase] its operation is implicit; it can have its occasion in interpretation, in doing history, in the confrontation of dialectic, but it does not constitute an explicit, established, universally recognised criterion of proper procedure in these specialties. (p. 268)

Now it is quite understandable why Lonergan should appeal for such openness. Benefit of clergy is a shaky basis for scholarly assertion, and in some areas blatantly absurd. A manuscript is a manuscript, and an archaeological discovery a discovery no matter who works on it. But as soon as scholarship involves agency, and not just passive, if competent, registering of data, the problem of relating functional expertise to human authenticity may be raised.

CONVERSION AS CRITERION?

The central difficulty about Lonergan's account is that the rôle of conversion as a *criterion* of proper procedure is circular and question-begging. If it is really to serve as a methodological criterion, conversion itself must be recognisable, and in some sense testable. Such tests as Lonergan offers, however, seem to succeed only by definition, or else to fail.

Take, for example, his account of intellectual conversion:

> Intellectual conversion is a radical clarification, and consequently the elimination of an exceedingly stubborn and misleading myth concerning reality, objectivity and human knowledge. The myth is that knowing is like looking, that objectivity is seeing what is there to be seen and not seeing what is not there, and that real is what is out there now to be looked at. (p. 234)

There are certainly good grounds for arguing a critical realist epistemology over against a naïve realist one, but is conversion really a *criterion* of truth in this issue? Lonergan uses the phrase 'intellectual conversion' as if it were equivalent of the rejection of naïve realism, empiricism, rationalism, idealism, positivism, pragmatism, phenomenology, existentialism. But if he really is doing this, he can no longer make conversion a criterion of the validity of such positions; for the rejection of such positions has been the identifying criterion of conversion itself. On the other hand there are no other concrete clues offered for identifying intellectual conversion. One simply has such unobjectionable, but vacuous, formal equivalents as that it is the discovery of 'the self-transcendence proper to the human process of coming to know: thus Lonergan unwittingly creates a dilemma: if one has an independent criterion of intellectual conversion, other than the holding of position X, it is too wide for Lonergan's purpose. Men of good intellectual faith, genuinely seeking the truth, have in fact come up with epistemologies other than critical realism. If, on the other hand, one makes the holding of position X the criterion of conversion, all he is doing by rejecting others as unconverted is reiterating a stipulative definition.

MORAL AND RELIGIOUS CONVERSION

The same difficulty arises, *mutatis mutandis,* with moral and religious conversion. If specific behaviour identifies the morally converted, an appeal to conversion cannot *warrant* the behaviour except at the cost of vicious circularity. On the other hand, if 'authenticity', moral or religious, has any existential correlates in terms of goodness or saintliness, these appear so regularly outside Christianity that they surely include more than Lonergan would want at the cognitive level.

He can, of course, account for this, much as the Ptolemaic system could accommodate the irregularities of planetary motion in terms of epicycles.[1] Men may be converted but have a consciousness which is less than fully differentiated. On page 272, Lonergan spells out the variable permutations of differentiated and undifferentiated consciousness, but it is difficult to see this as having more than mathematical cogency. How, for example, does a man whose consciousness is differentiated in the realms of theory, interiority, transcendence and art differ from one whose differentiations are in the realms of interiority, transcendence, scholarship and art? Do actual types correspond to the mathematical possibilities of double, treble, quadruple and quintuple differentiation? Are there ways of diagnosing areas of non-differentiation?

The examples Lonergan gives of insufficiently differentiated consciousness, for instance in the chapters on Foundations and Doctrines, hardly help. As with unconversion, such insufficiencies seem to be identified by the holding of unsatisfactory views, but no independent criterion for 'satisfactoriness' is offered. This is not immediately apparent because of the level of abstraction on which the book operates, and because of Lonergan's sophistication as a theologian. In the end, however, the circularity is staggering.

> In the world mediated by meaning and motivated by value, objectivity is simply the consequence of authentic subjectivity,

> of genuine attention, genuine intelligence, genuine reasonableness, genuine responsibility. (p. 265)

or

> The investigator will know from personal experience just what intellectual, moral and religious conversion is. He will have no great difficulty in distinguishing positions from counterpositions. . . . Moreover, all such investigators will tend to agree and, as well, they will be supported in part by other investigators that have been converted in one or two of the areas but not in all three. (p. 251)

or

> The criterion . . . [of whether one's insights are correct] . . . is whether or not one's insights are invulnerable, whether or not they hit the bull's eye, whether or not they meet *all* relevant questions so that there are no further questions that can lead to further insights. (p. 162)

This is particularly characteristic of the chapter on doctrines where one might have hoped, in some ways, to find the nub of Lonergan's criterion of truth. But again it eludes one in the form of references to a normativeness pertaining to dialectic and foundations, and dependent on the normativeness attributed to divine revelation, inspired scripture, or church doctrine.

THEOLOGICAL PLURALISM

It may indicate the subtle and eirenic ecumenicism of Lonergan's position that it is so comprehensive. There is, however, something philosophically alarming about a position which doesn't enable one to distinguish an unconverted man from one who is converted but culturally undifferentiated, or from one who is culturally differentiated, but in a different way. Such generous pluralism is a welcome change from the rigid exclusiveness of many theologies of the past, but as a method of identifying theological truth it is impotent. Of course one may in the end have no more 'objective' criterion than the shared sense of authenticity in a complex of life and doctrine communally explored in life-style and thought, with the kind of historical awareness which Lonergan has. But this does not to date in the history of Christianity seem to warrant the facility of Lonergan's optimism. For there are *rival*, self-authenticating communities, all convinced that they have achieved self-transcendence, and yet making competing truth claims. Of course from any one theological stance the others can be made sense of: they can be identified as wilful sinners, as predestinately damned, or more gently as undifferentiatedly conscious! But some fairly high-level coherence between intellectual, moral and spiritual realms, and considerable sophistication of consciousness seems to characterise most major world faiths, let alone divergent options within Christianity.

The force of Lonergan's pluralist account depends on his conviction that there are various ways of saying the same thing; or, more importantly, of *being* the same thing, since conversion is really a process of transformation. At the intellectual level, this is seen most clearly in the Doctrines section. The historicity of doctrines (expression) can be tolerated, and even welcomed, because it is intentionally related to the permanence of dogma (meaning). Or again, communications is seen basically as a translation exercise, in which the communicator works out cultural transpositions which are necessary, but which in some sense leave the identity of the faith intact.

That something is true independently of the believer's conviction that it is true is a presupposition of any realist philosophy. It is not Lonergan's confidence that objective (or self-transcendent) truth is to be found which is being challenged by this paper. What seems doubtful is the idea that one 'truth of meaning' can be identified in such manifold ongoing contexts as Lonergan suggests. Even to consider the norms he suggests, divine revelation, inspired scripture or church doctrine takes one into the heart of the problem. For many more people would acknowledge these as formal norms than would agree on their identification. The locus of divine revelation, the theological authority of scripture and the recognition of the true church are all as difficult to agree about as the doctrinal norms they have been variously supposed to sanction. Experience of the risen Christ, knowledge of the historical Jesus, inspiration by the Holy Spirit, and direct acquaintance with the Ultimate Reality, God, are equally problematic, and equally disputed.

The most radical question which must be put to Lonergan in this area is whether such a central identity of the faith as he implies can really be postulated. Of course, if faith is true, or appropriate, then God is, and God's identity is presumably intact. Further, if faith is understood as the intentional relation between man and

God, then that, by definition, is the common factor in all faith. But what, concretely, is their common faith may be virtually impossible to establish, and sceptical incredulity may therefore greet the claim that there is *anything* in common between them.

This problem is only fully appreciated in the context of world religions, but it is hardly necessary to move so far. In passing, however, it is worth noting that comparative religionists tend to doubt whether, phenomenologically speaking, there are strong grounds for believing that different religions basically 'believe the same thing'. On the whole, they tend to see that as a theological dogma belonging to some faiths, (Hinduism more characteristically than Christianity) and necessitated more by a doctrine of God or of Reality than by the appearances of the thing. Indeed Lonergan's account has some affinities with a vedantist account of theological disagreement.

> It may be objected that *nihil amatum nisi praecognitum*. But while that is true of other human love, [?] it need not be true of the love with which God floods our hearts through the Holy Spirit he has given us. That grace could be the finding that grounds our seeking God through natural reason and through positive religion. . . . Finally, it is in such grace that can be found the theological justification of Catholic dialogue with all Christians, with non-Christians, and even with atheists who may love God in their hearts while not knowing him with their heads.

This is a defensible theological position, albeit a controversial one. Its defence involves more than one of the functional specialties which Lonergan discusses, and as such it is a fairly typical theological question. Its defence, however, is not a matter of methodological consideration, and does not follow more necessarily from Lonergan's description of method than would a contrary position. The point hardly needs labouring, but one might indicate the key points of disagreement with an imagined opponent which prescriptions of method would not resolve.

First, there is the research relevant to this issue. Decisions about this may already indicate potential disagreement, but suppose that at least Scripture and other past Church pronouncements are held to deserve consideration. While elements in both suggest some possibility of a universally embracing relation between God and man, other elements in both seem to suggest that those outside the community which explicitly names Christ are excluded from that relationship. Such points would probably have to be conceded by exegetes and historians whatever their own Christian commitment, and whether or not they wished to endorse universalism themselves. The question becomes more difficult when one has to judge whether any given strand is central or peripheral. That is in part a descriptive question; there is some implausibility about affirming the centrality of a position which only a handful of people advocate. But it is certainly not a statistical question; a minority may defend a central doctrine; remnants may be faithful, and Athanasii may stand against worlds.

How then does one judge centrality? Perhaps in terms of how intimately the view coheres with the rest of one's theological convictions, theoretical and practical. Both positions, however, survive that test in different ways. One holds that the exclusivist strand is local, cultural conditioning, against which must be set the universalim of God's love disclosed in Jesus, and known in immediate moral conviction. The other claims that there is little evidence that clearly shows Jesus' position on the matter; and that if one takes Scripture seriously there is rather more evidence the other way. The moral argument is inconclusive, since agnosticism about *how* God's goodness relates to human ethical judgments is part of proper reverence, and that God may so transcend human ethics as to appear to contradict them. Indeed the problem of evil arises for any Christian, universalist or not. In practical attitudes there may be little to choose; the universalist may be freely accepting of all other men, or patronisingly insistent that it really is his God whom they know. The exclusivist may proselytise with belligerence, or may sympathetically try to share his faith by living it as attractively as possible. There is certainly no guarantee that one theoretical position goes with a better life-style than another.

Both might claim that their conviction on this matter is a function of their sense of 'being grasped by the love of God'. The universalist might then suggest that any account of goodness compatible with a notion of eternal damnation was not merely agnostic but equivocal; and the exclusivist could with some cogency reply that even universalist accounts of Providence run the same risk in view of the apparently appalling meaninglessness of some human lives.

Once the argument reaches this level it is hard to see what light

Method in Theology can shed on the situation. Of course it can suggest that, if words mean anything at all, both cannot be right. One or both, therefore, must be wrong. They may be misreading the data, or the consciousness of one or both may be insufficiently differentiated in some respect, or one or both may lack moral, intellectual or religious conversion. Apart from a general injunction to be aware of these possibilities, and to re-scrutinise the evidence, there is not much more Lonergan can suggest.

This is not a limitation he manifests alone. Most theologies which suggest foolproof criteria for detecting error seem not to do justice to the complexity of experience and understanding involved. In the end, no-one seems to get convincingly nearer than some kind of broad coherence which integrates reflection and experience and takes account of the data of past and present Christian reflection and experience in its self-understanding. All of these elements are ambiguous, however, since the judgment/decision about what data count as evidence, and how evidence should be weighted have no independently established criteria. Formally, authorities are authoritative only in so far as they participate in something like 'the charged field of love and meaning' which Lonergan identifies as the foundational criterion (p. 290). Diagnosing such participation, however, is a restatement of, not a solution to the problem. And claiming some kind of self-authenticating *Zusammenhalt* is hardly a criterion of truth, but the reiteration of a basic conviction, than which nothing is more basic in one's whole existence.

Lonergan's limitation is not that he fails to offer concrete modes of eliminating theological disagreement. It is that he appears to expect that he *can* do so by methodology, or, in his own words, to believe that 'the method is designed to take care of the matter'. This conviction seems structurally parallel to Kant's belief that the universalisability maxim led infallibly to the establishment of what was the right thing to do in concrete situations. Lonergan's position seems less crudely mistaken because of his awareness of and sensitivity to historical/cultural variables, but it is flawed in precisely the same way as Kant's. Thus, what one approaches hopefully as a prescription for doing theology turns out to be a surreptitiously circular formal description; proper theology is what is done by people employing proper procedures, being properly attentive, intelligent, reasonable and responsible, and having the proper differentiation of consciousness to articulate their conversion.

Obviously his recommendations are at points concrete enough to allow blatant kinds of errors to be corrected, e.g. wilful refusal to admit textual or historical evidence. But most of the interesting problems of theological disagreement are far more subtle than that. His account is also helpful in discrediting naïve views of objectivity which regard theological disagreement as a quasi-visual malfunctioning of one party or another, and that in itself makes some contribution to understanding the problem. His hope that *Method in Theology* will positively facilitate the overcoming of disagreement is hardly vindicated, however; except that disagreement with its own conclusions may presumably be put down to lack of some kind of conversion, or to insufficiently differentiated consciousness on the opponent's part.

In the end it is hard to be sure how much Lonergan thinks the overcoming of disagreement is a *desirable* objective. Certainly he wants unity of faith in the sense of universal radical conversion, and whatever can humanly be done to attain that objective (though it is divinely initiated) must be strenuously pursued. On cultural disagreement he is more ambiguous. He calls such differences 'benign', but whether this simply means 'non-malignant' or whether it means positively beneficial is not altogether clear. On the whole, the weight of his argument seems to suggest the former sense, as if disagreement were in some way undesirable though virtually inevitable and not a cause for panic. The shifting consciousness of historically conditioned men may afford permissible, though varying, accounts of the truth, but common meaning is ultimately that which is intentionally recognised and communally articulated. The variables of expression are not actually constitutive of the meaning of the faith.

> As common meaning constitutes community, so divergent meaning divides it. Such division may amount to no more than a diversity of culture and the stratification of individuals into classes of higher and lower competence. (p. 357)

Such a view begins by assuming common meaning as constitutive of community, and is forced to explain divergent meaning as incompetence or sin. Perhaps there is a theological alternative which is more challenging. Suppose one starts from the empirically-related conviction that men of much the same intellectual, moral and spiritual competence do disagree. What modifications of current understanding of God does this suggest, and is there any possibility of giving a constructive account of such divergence, rather than one which is merely non-pejorative? That is a question of enlarging on Lonergan's appreciation of pluralism, and seeing whether one can possibly make sense (theologically as well as sociologically) of *divergent* meaning as constitutive of community. Whether this should best be seen as an aspect of theodicy, or as an aspect of a theology of culture is an open question, though both areas are involved. At any rate, the concentration of the functional expertise of the various specialists Lonergan identifies might well be applied to this range of problems as a way of recognising the intention of good-will which *Method in Theology* indicates.

As far as the functional specialties go, criticism of Lonergan's precise account should not obscure the importance of the area. Many theological disputes presuppose disagreement about the interrelatedness of different branches of theological expertise. Is it a matter of faith that the conclusions of the exegete and those of the systematic theologian should never clash? But what procedures must be followed if they do? It is not merely a hypothetical possibility that New Testament scholars and early church historians cast doubt, for example, on the Dominical institution of sacraments, or the Biblical ground of Trinitarian doctrines. But not enough work has been done on the question of interrelation between such findings and established doctrines. Does the 'proper openness' which Lonergan advocates imply in principle that doctrine could be undermined by exegetical or historical findings? Or does doctrinal conviction, for example, of the Trinitarian structure of God enable one to resist New Testament scholarship which suggests that such convictions misread the evidence?

There are many such issues in contemporary theology which do not fall in the province of any one specialist, but lie between them, in a zone which requires methodological mapping, or theological exploration, or both, since the two are properly inseparable. Whatever the defects of the account under consideration, Lonergan pinpoints some of the areas which most demand theological attention in our contemporary situation if constructive advances are to be made.

NOTE
1 An analogy adapted from John Hick's unpublished paper, 'Towards a Christian Theology of other Religions': Society for the Study of Theolog, Lancaster, 1973.

History and Meaning in Bernard Lonergan's Approach to Theological Method

Wolfhart Pannenberg

MEANING

In his book, *Method in Theology* (1972), Lonergan presents a detailed account of the task of theology on the basis of what he calls 'transcendental method' which was developed earlier in his study of human understanding entitled *Insight* (1957). There he distinguished four operations of the knowing subject: sense experience, intellectual inquiry and insight, rational reflection and judgment, responsible evaluation and decision, and this hierarchy of operations is now applied to theology. But in order to do so, Lonergan first explores the phenomenon of religion, and he approaches this phenomenon through the human concern for the human good and within the context of meaning.[1] It is not quite clear how these two aspects are related to each other within Lonergan's concept of religion. But it seems that in his view the 'drive to value' (35) is embedded in the context of 'our conscious intentionality' (103) which produces the meaning that mediates the world to us. The highest 'realm of meaning', beyond common sense and theoretical knowledge, is constituted, according to Lonergan, by the conversion of the mind from those 'outer realms' to 'one's own interiority, one's subjectivity, one's operations, their structure, their norms, their potentialities' (83). And it is by adverting to our own questioning that the question of God arises (103), because 'the question of God is implicit in all our questioning', and 'being in love with God is the basic fulfilment of our conscious intentionality' (105).

The approach to religion by way of the phenomenon of meaning is a distinctive characteristic not only of Lonergan's way of dealing with religion, but of many recent investigations in this subject matter. Especially sociologists from Durkheim to Parsons, Luckmann, Berger and Luhmann have equated religion with the most comprehensive conception of meaning that forms the basis of all social life in a given society. And in his book, *Meaning and Method* (1972), Anders Nygren reformulated his ideas on theological method in the context of a theory of meaning. Nygren's book shows some interesting similarities with Lonergan's, especially in the point that Nygren, too, advocates a transcendental method in theology. But while Lonergan's transcendentalism consists in an application of a general analysis of knowledge to the special field of theology, Nygren envisages a particular transcendental root of religion, a *religious a priori*, and he accordingly assumes a particularly religious 'realm of meaning'. In Lonergan, the distinction of various realms of meaning means quite a different thing: he does not refer to different functions of the mind and correspondingly different realms of reality, but to different 'stages' of our 'conscious intentionality' in terms of common sense, theory and interiority. Behind this, there is a different understanding of meaning. The discussion on the connectedness of meaning and religion requires in the first place clarification of the different ways to use the term 'meaning'. In the case of Nygren, the use of the term is related to the discussions of analytical philosophy. The hermeneutical tradition of Schleiermacher and Dilthey suggests another idea of meaning. In Lonergan, again, the term 'meaning' refers to a different phenomenon.

In Nygren's work as in Wittgenstein's *Philosophical Investigations*, the 'meaning' of a word is determined by the context, in the first instance by the sentence, but also by the broader context of speech. This is also the point of departure of the hermeneutical theory of meaning. But while Wittgenstein in his model of 'language games' thought of a *typical* context of the use of words and could ask, therefore, for *rules* which determine the use of words in that context, and while Nygren transposes this way of analysis to his transcendental method of an 'analysis of presuppositions' of different contexts of meaning, the hermeneutical conception of meaning as contextuality focuses on the individual and the unique, historical context. In addition, the hermeneutical approach to meaning is less concerned with the reference of words to objects, but extends to the interpretation of particulars in relation to the whole of their context beyond the interpretation of literary documents to a general analysis of the historicity of human experience. In contrast to both these theories of meaning, in Lonergan's work the concept of meaning is not constituted by the relatedness of particulars to their context.

In Lonergan's perspective, meaning is not primarily the *objective content* of a particular experience, insofar as experience perceives the *significance* of its objects, but an *act* of the subject, 'an act of conceiving, thinking, considering, defining, supposing, formulating', and in its full sense an act of judging (74).[2] Certainly, the act of meaning is related to a something that is meant. Lonergan calls this the 'term' of meaning.[3] The term of meaning, however, is taken only as correlate of the 'act' that somebody 'means' something and as constituted by that act. This suggests a theory of meaning in terms of intentionality: 'For what is meant, is what is intended in questioning . . .' (77). 'Meaning, when fully developed, intends something meant' (62).

It can be said, then, that in contrast to the theory of meaning as reference which prevails in logical positivism and in linguistic semantics, and to the theory of meaning as contextuality which the later Wittgenstein and hermeneutical philosophy have in common, Lonergan follows the theory of meaning as intentionality which can be traced back to E. Husserl. It is interesting that Lonergan approvingly refers to Husserl's analysis of intentionality (212), especially because he takes Husserl's distinction of the logical structure of intentionality from psychological acts for a mere addition of an objective reference beyond the subjective immanence of psychological phenomena. Thus we have in Lonergan as in much contemporary sociology (following M. Weber) a psychologizing interpretation of Husserl's idea of meaning as intentionality.[4]

This could be irreproachable in itself. But it constitutes a problem that Lonergan shows no awareness of the fact that there are other theories of meaning which should be taken seriously and the truth of which should be incorporated even in the case of a decision for a theory of meaning in terms of intentionality. Especially, there is not the slightest indication of the fact that there are important positions — Wittgenstein and hermeneutical philosophy — which take meaning to be dependent on a given context of language and/ or behaviour and experience. Although later in Lonergan's book the idea of context becomes rather important, it is not present — strangely enough — in his chapter on meaning.

CONTEXT AND HISTORY

In an important way the term 'context' appears first in connection with the task of interpretation (155).[5] Here, Lonergan emphasizes the methodological importance of reconstructing the context of a word in order to determine its 'actual meaning' in distinction from its 'heuristic meaning', which one may find in a dictionary and use at the beginning of the investigation (163). Similarly, the chapter on history emphasizes at least on one occasion (183) the importance of the context of events for determining their significance, although on the other hand history is said to be constituted ('in part') by 'acts' of meaning.[6] In the entire section (181 ff) the peculiar character of historical investigation, as it was analysed by Droysen or Dilthey or Collingwood, is beautifully characterized without however realizing its implications concerning a dependence of the significance of the parts on the whole. Only in summarizing the position of others, especially of Droysen, does Lonergan parallel 'meaning and significance' as revealing 'the proper reality' of events within their particular contexts and mentions that the facts of history 'resemble . . . the meaning of a text' (199). Here, of course, the term 'meaning' does not refer to the intentionality of human acts, but to the dependence of something particular on its context.

In general, however, this structure of meaning which is the object of 'understanding' in Dilthey's sense, is not in the focus of Lonergan's book. Because he takes 'meaning' in the narrower sense of intentionality, the search for meaning can become the privilege of the exegete in contrast to the historian: 'It is not, of course, the historian's but the exegete's task to determine what was meant' (178). The question is whether history and exegesis can be separated as neatly as this statement suggests. Is it not necessary to explore the historical context of the situation of the author's formulation of his text in order to interpret correctly the kind of intention which the author himself was expressing by his words? And is it not necessary, in addition, to explore also the historical conditions, why a given text meant to those who read it something other than the author intended? 'We very often mean what we do not mean; i.e. we refer to what we do not intend.'[7] This aspect of the phenomenon of meaning obviously escapes the interpretation of meaning as intentional.

It is only because he takes for granted the interpretation of meaning in terms of intentionality, that Lonergan thinks himself in a position to dismiss rather shortly the hermeneutical idea of understanding (*Verstehen*) as it was developed by Dilthey and as it is widely used in contemporary hermeneutical philosophy and theology. Lonergan dismisses the claim that understanding in this sense is a fundamental characteristic of the procedures in all humanities, and he does so by affirming that his own use of the term insight and understanding is 'more precise and has a broader range than the connotation and denotation of *Verstehen*' (212). Unfortunately, Lonergan does not offer in this context any further argument, why and in what respect his own idea of understanding is superior to the hermeneutical concept of understanding. It seems as if he has not become aware of the fact that the hermeneutical idea of understanding (*Verstehen*) belongs to a theory of meaning different from his own, a theory of the historicity of human experience in terms of the correlativity of parts and wholes: we cannot understand a particular event except in relation to the particular context within which it occurred.

UNDERSTANDING

According to Lonergan's philosophy, understanding belongs to a particular stage or 'level' of the cognitional process: it mediates between the data on one hand and reflective judgment on the other.[8] There are sensible data and data of consciousness.[9] Common to both is that they represent what is given to the mind and not a product of its own activity, although the data of consciousness consist of the operations of the mind itself. What is given, then, 'supplies ... the raw materials on which intelligence operates':[10] inquiry into the data yields insights grasping a unity in the data,[11] either the concrete unity of a thing or abstract unities like laws. This level of intelligence or 'understanding', however, is to be complemented by a further level, that of rationality[12] or reflection[13] asking 'whether such understanding and formulation are correct'.[14] To this question the act of judgment corresponds which 'answers that they are or are not'.[15] It becomes possible by taking the formulation of an insight as conditioned and as 'virtually unconditioned' in case it fulfils the conditions applying to it.[16]

The sharp separation of understanding as attainment of insight from the data that are understood and from the reflective question as to the correctness of such understanding is not convincing. Gestalt psychology and linguistic analysis[17] have demonstrated that perception is not related to 'data', but to things. Lonergan, however, although he is aware of the abstract character of the term 'sensation',[18] speaks of a continuous attention to the 'flow of sensations' as leading to understanding[19] which comprises the perception of things as well as the insight into abstract patterns. But is it not only by an act of reflection that we distinguish our perception of things from 'data' which are integrated into the unity of such a perception?[20] Thus, in Lonergan's distinction between the first two 'levels' of the cognitional process we might have a reification of that subsequent reflection rather than simply a description of the cognitional process.

INSIGHT AND REFLECTION

More plausible seems the distinction between direct insight and reflection. Nevertheless, the particular form of that distinction remains objectionable: is it really first by reflection that the element of truth or correctness is added[21] to insight and understanding? Does not every insight and, indeed, every perception implicitly claim truth and correctness? Does not reflection, then, by considering whether a formulation or an insight is correct or not, merely render explicit what was implicit in direct experience, in perception and insight? Thus, the distinction between reflection and direct insight seems to be characterized by the relation between implication and explication rather than by 'additions' of the former to the latter.

Furthermore, reflection does not only concern the correctness of an insight or of a perception, but *all sorts* of implications in them. Lonergan himself emphasizes that sensations do not occur in isolation, but within a context or 'flow' of others. Now, sensation in itself is an artifical concept. But the same contextual character holds true for all experience. Lonergan even speaks of a 'contextual aspect of judgment'.[22] For each judgment there is 'a context of other judgments that determine its meaning'.[23] How do we become aware of those contexts if not by reflection? Is it not by reflection that Lonergan himself constructs in his work 'a series of disparate contexts' in order to comprise them within an 'upper context'?[24] And does not his construction claim to provide the *appropriate* context for the phenomena under discussion? Does not his reflective construction, then, try to render explicit the context of meaning which is implicit in the matters that appeared at first in isolation?

But if reflection has to do with an explication of the context implicit in the phenomenon reflected upon, how is this to be related to the reflection upon the *conditions* of an insight which, according to Lonergan, leads to judgment? Is not the entire concrete context of a phenomenon or of the occurrence of a perception or of a linguistic expression contributing to its conditions?

This seems to contradict Lonergan's assertion that each judgment is 'a limited commitment', limited 'to affirm some single conditioned that has a finite number of conditions which, in fact, are fulfilled' (345). If the judgment is in fact conditioned by the concrete context of its object as well as of itself, then the number of its conditions is infinite. Each individual judgment, then, presupposes an anticipation of the universe.

Lonergan has called this position that of relativist thought (342 ff.), which he characterizes by the assumption that the universe is 'a tissue of internal relations' and hence 'no part and no aspect of the universe can be known in isolation from any other part or aspect' (344). Against that perspective and its consequence that all judgments are open to revision, he calls upon the definitive character of individual judgments like 'this is a typewriter', and he claims that this definitive character of individual judgments 'results from the combination of a conditioned with the fulfilment of its conditions' (344). But this would work only on the assumption that the number of the conditions is limited or reducible to first principles, and there is no reason for such an assumption if the conditions for any particular phenomenon are to be discovered in its concrete context. How, then, are individual judgments possible at all? Only by an anticipation of the universe which may occur in different forms and be refuted in the process of further experience. Lonergan says that the individual judgment is not 'pronouncing on the universe', but on 'some single conditioned' (345), and he is right in insisting on this point. But this is no objection, because the anticipation of the universe in most individual judgments is only implicit and belongs to its own conditions that can be uncovered only by a hermeneutical process of reflection and interpretation and reflection upon interpretation and further reinterpretation. However, what about the definitive character of judgments like 'this is a typewriter'? Why would it be 'silly', indeed (346), 'to doubt whether or not this is a typewriter'? Because of the conventional element in the use of words. A serious question for judgment occurs first, if it is asked whether some object is identical with what is commonly called a typewriter. In that case, contrary to Lonergan's assumption (347), neither the question for truth, nor the question for facts are banished. But the decision on what is to be considered matter of fact depends on assumptions concerning truth, and both can be known only by an anticipation which remains open for revision.

Lonergan charges the contextual analysis of knowledge with relativism, because he thinks that it leaves no room either for facts or for truth. But this is not so, although it belongs to the historicity of truth that all insights and judgments remain hypothetical. He is right, however, in suspecting that in such a perspective there is no independence of judgments or of assumptions about facts from the process of understanding.[25] Particulars are never conceived except within a context of understanding that conditions the very meaning of the particularity. The difference beten insights and data belongs to a secondary reflection which, of course, is not arbitrary, but corresponds to the objective intention of any insight or cognitive statement. This reflection and the judgment based upon it concerning the relations between an asserted insight and its relevant data do not, however, transcend understanding, because they render explicit previous understanding and themselves express new understanding. The decisive point is that reflection is not something foreign to understanding, that on the contrary all understanding involves some degree of reflective awareness, and the process of reflection renders explicit the implications of previous understanding. Nor is reflection leading beyond understanding: Lonergan himself indicates this by speaking of 'reflective understanding'[26] in addition to direct insight. He fails, however, to account sufficiently for the continuity of reflective understanding with 'understanding' in his more restricted use of the term.

If reflection and understanding belong together, then there is no point in accusing hermeneutical philosophy of being insufficiently aware of the 'third level of cognitional activity', i.e., reflection and judgment.[27] Rather, there arise serious dobuts about the adequacy of the sequence of three distinct 'levels' in Lonergan's 'transcendental method'. These doubts have consequences also for the scheme of functional specialties in Lonergan's *Method in Theology,* since that scheme is explicitly based on his model of the cognitional process: to the sequence of data, understanding, judgment corresponds the sequence of research, interpretation, history.[28] Again, the continuous process of reflective understanding is divided into 'levels'. But there is no definite priority of 'research' over against interpretation of texts and historical investigation. Nor is interpretation adequately achieved without historical knowledge. Lonergan himself speaks — in marked deviation from the scheme of his earlier book — of an 'interdependence' of the different specialties.[29] But why, then, is such a division needed at all? The argument that 'these branches of theological activity' represent 'distinct and separable stages in a single process from data to ultimate results'[30] is somewhat debilitated by the later concession that there is interdependence between them. There remains the fact that at least interpretation and history have come to be represented in theology by different disciplines, biblical exegesis and ecclesiastical history. But this fact is not to be explained by some correspondence to different phases in general cognitional process, but by historical circumstance, especially by the fundamental role of the authority of Scripture in the Christian tradition, while Church history became an independent discipline only since the quarrels about ecclesiastical traditions in the sixteenth century. Besides, while scriptural exegesis has been done for centuries with a minimum of historical knowledge and research, but today depends heavily on both, ecclesiastical history like general history is not conceivable without interpretation of documents and other evidence. In principle, therefore, interpretation and documentary research can be considered functions of historical knowledge because of the historicity of all understanding.

DIALECTIC

In the fourth place after research, interpretation and history, Lonergan introduces a discipline of dialectic which is to replace the older controversial theology by a treatment of the conflicts between Christians in a more ecumenical spirit.[31] This discipline corresponds to the fourth stage in Lonergan's scheme of the development of consciousness which through perception of data, understanding, judgment finally aims at personal 'decision' which in distinction from judgment represents the exercise of ethical freedom under the demand for 'consistency between his knowing and his deciding and doing.'[32] Accordingly, theological dialectic is assigned the task of tracing back the conflicts in Christianity to different ultimate decisions or conversions[33] which are said to constitute mutually exclusive 'horizons'.³⁴ 'Horizons' are said to comprise 'all our intentions, statements, deeds' (237), and 'dialectically opposed horizons lead to opposed value judgments, opposed accounts of historical movements, opposed interpretations of authors, and different selections of relevant data in special research' (247). In case of such 'a gross difference of horizon' the 'proportionate remedy' for conflict 'is nothing less than a conversion' (246).

One wonders how people who are imprisoned in such different horizons could communicate at all. It is certainly true that in many cases communication is extremely difficult. But Lonergan's theory of horizons would confine individuals to separate worlds except for some decision for conversion, which scarcely could be called rational any longer, because it lacks the possibility of motivation within a coherent horizon.

However, this problem arises perhaps only because of a peculiarly frozen idea of 'horizon': are horizons really that stiff and iron? Do they not rather move together with ourselves as we walk or drive on?³⁵ Horizons can broaden, they can shrink, they can diverge and they can merge. They are fixed only with somebody who no longer gets moving himself. Thus, the concept of horizon offers an excellent model of the historicity of human experience.

The isolation and — in extreme cases — opposition of horizons becomes a problem in Lonergan's thought, because in his view horizons are constituted by 'constitutive and effective acts of meaning' which provide the subject of an 'evaluative hermeneutics' (245). Here, the conception of meaning as intentionality leads to a constitution of meaning by decision. Lonergan's principle of interiority is coloured, at this point, by subjectivism.³⁶

AUTHORITY AND SUBJECTIVE DECISION

The importance of this idea of intentional decision constituting the horizon of experience for Lonergan's scheme as a whole becomes apparent, if one considers that there follows a second phase of theological specialties, but this time in reverse order: foundations correspond to decision,'doctrines to judgment, systematics to understanding, and communications to data. This indicates nothing less than that the entire sequence of disciplines in the second group is based upon conversion (268). The first of them, foundations, is to replace 'the old fundamental theology' by presenting on the basis of conversion 'the horizon within which the meaning of doctrines can be apprehended' (131). The following disciplines — doctrines, systematics, communications — only develop what is rooted in conversion. The horizon which originates from that decision is, however, not 'purely private'. It rather belongs to a social group which the individual joins (269). Therefore, Lonergan's model of theology does not only rest on personal decision, but also on authority as the chapter on doctrines reveals (295 ff.). The result seems to be a well-known combination of subjectivism and authority which is characteristic of so much of Protestant theology, especially in the more conservative brand of the pietistic tradition. That combination gives evidence of the fact that in the context of modern thought doctrinal authority is no longer acceptable on the basis of rational judgment — a judgment of credibility — as was the case in the medieval world, but only on the basis of a subjective decision that lacks the corroboration by argument it formerly enjoyed.

The dangerous implication of this modern trend of the self-understanding of theology is that the truth of authority itself becomes a function of a more or less arbitrary subjective decision. The divine truth, then, that faith relies upon falls back on the decision of the subject itself. The alternative to that way in modern theology has been to let theology be discussed without reservations in the context of critical rationality. Lonergan's principle of subjectivity or interiority could have pointed in that direction as well as his concept of religion based on the idea of meaning. But the analysis of meaning, because of the assumption that meaning is constituted by intentionality, renders meaning dependent on subjective decision. The consequence is that the analysis of meaning cannot be followed through to inter-subjectivity. This would require a priority of meaning over against the subject who experiences meaning. Such a priority of meaning over subjectivity as a basis for intersubjective unity of meaning is articulated by the analysis of the historicity of meaning in terms of the relativity of parts to wholes: because an individual experiences himself related to a whole more comprehensive than himself, he can identify others as related to the same context, and vice versa. Such intersubjective meaning always involves religion — not as acceptance of some revelational authority, but rather as an implication of all ordinary experience. For definite significance, attributed to particular occasions of experience, is constituted not only by its immediate context, but finally by the universe of meaning — even if it is regarded as an open question still what the universe of meaning may be like and what reality constitutes the unity of that universe. The universe of meaning, however, is manifested for us by those phenomena which comprehensively illuminate our experience so as to integrate the different elements and aspects of individual and social experience into a unified whole. This in itself represents no more than an anticipation of the universe of meaning which is still incomplete in the midst of an ongoing process of experience. But as we live on with it, it may prove itself by constantly illuminating and integrating the changing world of our experiences.

NOTES

1. Darton, Longman and Todd, London 1972, 25. The following page numbers in the text refer to this work.
2. Cf. *Method* 78, 92, 245. See also *Insight: A Study of Human Understanding* (Longmans, London 1958) 305.
3. 'A term of meaning is what is meant' — *Method* 75, cf. 92.
4. This comes also to expression in the procedure of Lonergan's chapter on meaning in that he treats (contrary to the method of language analysis) linguistic meaning as something secondary: 'Linguistic meaning is objective. It expresses what has been objectified. But the meaning of the smile is intersubjective' (60). The objective character of linguistic meaning seems to explain why Lonergan in this chapter does not start with language, but with prelinguistic expressions of meaning like the smile: this might have appeared to be more easily accounted for in terms of an act of a subject than the complex phenomenon of language.
5. But cf. 82, where it is said that the need for a systematic order of experience leads beyond common sense to the development of theories which provide a context for answers which arise from experience.
6. *Method* 179, cf. the attribution of meaning to the sphere of human life in analogy to the way law is attributed to nature (80 f.). The cumulative development as a distinctive character of history (81) comes also to expression in a description of the process of the conquest of America by the white men: 'The whole of that added, man-made, artificial world is the cumulative, now planned, now chaotic, product of human acts of meaning' (78). Here, the whole is the result of the cumulative addition of individual 'acts' of meaning instead of providing the horizon that first allows to determine the definite meaning of each contributing event or 'act'.
7. C. K. OGDEN and I. A. RICHARDS *The Meaning of Meaning* (1923, 8th ed. as Harvest Book 29, Hartcourt) 194 f.
8. *Method* 10, cf. *Insight* 272 ff. The subtitle of the book (A Study of Understanding), however, expresses a more comprehensive idea of understanding as referring to the entire process of cognition (cf. also *Insight* XXVII f. and the supplementation of 'direct understanding' by introspective and reflective understanding, *ibid.* 279 ff. and by 'unrestricted understanding', *ibid.* 644 ff.).
9. *Method* 201 f., *Insight* 72 ff., 274.

10 *Insight* 273.
11 *Ibid.* 481, cf. X, also 274 where Lonergan affirms that it is 'the attitude of the inquiring mind that effects the transition from the first level to the second', and 338: 'inquiry leading from the given to insight'.
12 *Insight* 322 ff.
13 *Ibid.* 273.
14 *Ibid.* 275, cf. also 279.
15 *Ibid.* cf. 271 ff.
16 *Ibid.* 338, cf. 280 f., 671 f. Thus 'reasonableness is reflection inasmuch as it seeks groundedness for objects of thought' (323).
17 As to the latter, see J. L. AUSTIN, *Sense and Sensibilia* (ed. G. J. Warnock, Oxford U.P. 1962).
18 *Insight* 181. It is because of the contextual character of experience that Lonergan calls it abstract 'to speak of a sensation'.
19 *Insight* 73 f., cf. the correspondence of 'perceptual images' to data (274) in distinction from insights which arise from inquiring into them.
20 Cf. *Insight* 246.
21 *Insight* 275: 'The cognitional process is thus a cumulative process; later steps presuppose earlier contributions and add them.'
22 *Ibid.* 276, cf. 375 f.
23 *Ibid.* 325 (in this context does the term 'meaning' refer to intentionality?).
24 *Ibid.* 731. The subsequent page numbers in the text refer to *Insight*.
25 *Insight* 343 ff., *Method* 213.
26 *Insight* 279 ff.
27 *Method* 213.
28 *Ibid.* 135.
29 *Ibid.* 141 ff.
30 *Ibid.* 136. The discussion on the following page (137) even suggests that each discipline has its own independent 'principles'.
31 *Ibid.* 129 f.
32 *Insight* 613.
33 *Method* 237 ff.
34 *Ibid.* 236 f., 247 ff. Subsequent page numbers in the text refer to *Method*.
35 See H. G. GADAMER, *Wahrheit und Methode* (J. C. B. Mohr, Tübingen 1962) 288.
36 Lonergan himself, to be sure, emphasizes that 'a deliberate decision is anything but arbitrary' (*Method* 268). It is 'a high achievement' (269), because most people 'do not advert to the multiplicity of horizons', but 'merely drift into some contemporary horizon' (*ibid.*). But would not deliberate choice presuppose reasoning and reasoning a continuous horizon within which it develops? Lonergan's description of 'migrating from the one they have inherited to another they have discovered to be better' (*ibid.*) is hardly conceivable without the assumption of a mediating horizon comprehending both, the starting point in the old one and the goal within the new. The closest Lonergan approaches to the notion of changing horizons is, later on, his idea of an 'ongoing context of church doctrines' (313). Even this movement, however, seems to represent, in his view, rather a development within one and the same horizon.

The Function of Inner and Outer Word in Lonergan's Theological Method

T. F. Torrance

THE WORD

By the word is meant any expression of religious meaning or of religious value. Its carrier may be intersubjectivity, or art, or symbol, or language, or the remembered and portrayed lives or deeds or achievements of individuals or classes or groups. Normally all modes of expression are employed but, since language is the vehicle in which meaning becomes most fully articulated, the spoken and written word are of special importance in the development and clarification of religion.

By its word, religion enters the world mediated by meaning and regulated by value. It endows that world with its deepest meaning and its highest value. It sets itself in a context of other meanings and other values. Within that context it comes to understand itself, to relate itself to the object of ultimate concern, to draw on the power of ultimate concern to pursue the objectives of proximate concern all the more fairly and all the more efficaciously.

Before it enters the world mediated by meaning, religion is the prior word God speaks to us by flooding our hearts with his love. That prior word pertains, not to the world mediated by meaning, but to the world of immediacy, to the unmediated experience of the mystery of love and awe. The outwardly spoken word is historically conditioned: its meaning depends upon the human context in which it is uttered, and such contexts vary from place to place and from one generation to another. But the prior word in its immediacy, though it differs in intensity, though it resonates differently in different temperaments and in different stages of religious development, withdraws man from the diversity of history by moving out of the world mediated by meaning and towards a world of immediacy in which image and symbol, thought and word, lose their relevance and even disappear.[1]

This notion of the word represents Fr. Lonergan's appropriation of the Augustinian-Thomist concept of the inner word, and its outer expression, and its transposition into what he regards as the modern world of meaning and history as it has come to be affected by a vast reorientation in science and philosophy, shifting the focus of interest to the national self-consciousness or critical interiority of the human subject. In its mediaeval roots this differs rather sharply from Anselm's basic concept of the word (*proprium et principale rei verbum*) which, whether in our inward thinking or outward speaking of it, is directed immediately at the 'solid' reality its signifies and is therefore to be understood in accordance with the nature of that reality and not some intermediate mental event. In its modern form, significantly, it differs no less sharply from Karl Barth's concept of the word at much the same point, where, in the interest of a scientific theology operating objectively on its own proper ground, Barth had to part company with the modern turn to a phenomenological approach and indeed to an anthropological and subjective starting-point which has characterised Neo-Protestantism so widely. Unfortunately, Lonergan's knowledge of the thought of Anselm (not to mention Duns Scotus!) seems to be as inexact as his knowledge of the thought of Barth is scanty (to say the least!), but if we are to do justice to Lonergan's own position and appreciate the distinctive slant he gives to the notion of the inner and outer word we must examine his thought in the context of his methodological intention and in the light of the horizon-shifts he has sought to carry through.

THE ESSENTIAL TASK OF THEOLOGY

The essential problem for theology, as Lonergan sees it, is twofold. One the one hand, theology is confronted with the claim that 'all other sciences than the mathematical have the name of science only by courtesy',[2] which is no less the case with modern empirical science than it was with classical essentialist science. In this situation theology finds itself demoted from being a science to being merely an academic discipline where its rank in the pecking order is assigned according to its 'success'.

> Some third way, then, must be found and, even though it is difficult and laborious, that price must be paid if the less successful subject is not to remain a mediocrity or slip into decadence and desuetude.[3]

On the other hand, theology is confronted today by a new world of constitutive and effective meaning brought about by a quite different, dynamic kind of science leading to a new science of man, that is, a world which is not only known but created, for knowing is itself a dynamic and structural process, and a correlative understanding of human reality as in large measure constituted through acts of meaning.[4] Here, then, theology must adapt itself to the fact that the classical mediation of meaning has broken down, and is being replaced by another, geared to the self-constitutive nature of the human understanding, and thus learn to operate within modern culture in which meaning takes precedence over the reality meant and intelligibility is not so much something that is found as what is consciously and actively intended by the intelligent subject.

Lonergan's methodological concern, therefore, is to work out a basis for his projected *third way* for theology between exact, mathematical sciences and merely academic disciplines, within the horizon-shift from classical science concerned with certain knowledge grounded in universal and necessary truths to empirical science concerned with hypothetical knowledge reached through freely chosen postulates, and from a world of theoretical penetration into the interrelations of objects or things among themselves to a world of interiorly differentiated consciousness which becomes disclosed in the actual processes of knowing. What Lonergan attempts to come up with is a general science transcending all the special sciences and the specific methods they develop with reference to the determinate conditions of the fields into which they inquire, and which therefore holds good for every science and discipline. In the classical world such a general science had to do with being as being, but in the modern world, he claims, it has to do with the data of consciousness, and the procedures of the human mind discerned behind the procedures of the natural sciences.[5]

These two sets of procedures operate like the upper and lower blades of a pair of shears, but whereas the procedures that constitute the lower blade vary with the different methodical modes developed in the special sciences in accordance with the distinctive natures and material conditions of each field, the procedures which constitute the upper blade are disclosed through analysis to embody structural and dynamic features which recur in all human cognitional activity. They are not structures deriving from what is known but are invariant structures immanent and operative in all knowing, independent of and irrespective of the nature or condition of the field in question. As such they are not open to radical revision for they are the condition of the possibility of any revision — a revision of these structures would be a rejecting of itself. While in themselves these structures are empty, they nevertheless anticipate a form that is to be filled in and thus perform a heuristic function in the advance of human knowledge. What is more, however, they settle in advance the general determinations, not merely of the activities of knowledge, but also of the content of the known, and thus form the necessary pre-condition for the fundamental validity of knowledge in any science or discipline. On the other hand, Fr. Lonergan argues, these dynamic heuristic structures immanent in human cognitional activity are not discovered by some sort of Platonic reminiscence but are disclosed only through reductive analysis of the actual operations of knowledge in the special science.[6]

TRANSCENDENTAL METHOD

This, then, is Lonergan's *third way,* reached with the discovery of a basic pattern of operations employed in every cognitional activity. He speaks of it as a *transcendental method*. It is transcendental in that it is independent of all particular scientific contents and invariant over all culture, and transcendental also in the sense that it brings to light the conditions of the possibility of knowing an object in so far as that knowledge is *a priori*.[7] It is a transcendental deployment of the common core and ground of the methods appropriate to particular fields but which in the independent and explicit self-consciousness of the reason retains an open heuristic character. As a method, then, it is not a set of rules, but a prior normative pattern of recurrent and related operations consciously and dynamically deployed to yield cumulative and progressive results. Thus Lonergan lays immense stress upon *intentionality* in which the human subject 'makes objects present' to himself, and 'objectifies the contents of what he intends', yet in such a way that he breaks through merely categorial determination of objects in a dynamic heuristic operation which keeps the intentional act open to further advance, pressing it beyond what he knows to seek to what he does not yet know. It is characteristic of Lonergan's 'method', however, that it requires the focus of attention to be transferred to the consciously intending subject in a deliberate attempt on his part to heighten the consciousness of his intending by objectifying it for himself, so that he may learn what the conscious operations of his mind are and learn to act in explicit consciousness of its inherent norms, structures and procedures. In this way the self-structuring nature of the human understanding is thematised into a 'scientific method' which applies to all fields: it is the conative deployment of the invariant structures of the consciousness as a normative pattern in the control of meaning, through which the real world is mediated to us, replacing the classical control of meaning by theoretical penetration into the structured interrelations of things in themselves. Such a scientific method through 'self-appropriation' is 'the third way' which Lonergan projects for theology, with primacy given to the upper blade of the heuristic method in the invariant structures of the theologian's consciousness, and with a vast shift in emphasis from insight into intrinsic intelligibility to insight that shapes experience and dynamic meaning as constitutive of reality, i.e. to the active correlate of intelligibility. Such a transcendental method is admittedly only a part of theological method, but it supplies 'the basic anthropological component'[8] necessary for its critical, foundational, normative, heuristic and other functions, in unity with inquiry in all other fields. Its specifically religious component comes from its transcendent ground in God,[9] but nevertheless on Lonergan's showing it is the cognitional structure of the intending religious subject that determines the general nature and basic patterns of his knowledge, for the objective pole of his knowing is not God as such but the meanings through which he is mediated and becomes 'reality' for the intending subject.

Quite evidently, this whole concept of method presupposes that the pattern of relations immanent in the structure of cognitional acts corresponds to or is identical with the pattern of relations in the ontological structure of the reality known, for otherwise the latter could not be known through the former, nor could the former play any anticipatory or heuristic, far less any normative, rôle in relation to the latter. Thus, Fr. Lonergan readily grants that his cognitional theory rests upon the major premise of 'the isomorphism that obtains between the structure of knowing and the structure of the known'.[10] The way in which Lonergan conceives this, however, not just as a reflection of the known, nor merely as a correlation to it that arises in and with the operational activities of inquiry, but as grounded in a relation not of confrontation but of identity between the contents of cognitional acts with the known, or identity between the dynamic structure of knowing and the structure of its proportionate known,[11] allows him to claim for the invariant structures of the mind an explanatory anticipation of the invariant structure of reality proportionate to human cognitional activity.[12] Moreover, although they are disclosed only through reductive analysis of the methodological operations of the sciences, these invariant structures of the mind are conceived as prescinding entirely from material scientific content, as features independently inherent in the human understanding. This has the effect of giving those structures a strong psychological and volitional slant which enables Lonergan to use them, not simply as a methodical constant, but in a constitutive and creative way which reverses the positions of the intending subject and the objective pole, and therefore of transcendental method and the determinate method of a special science. That is to say, Lonergan's thought takes a distinctively subjectivist turn, but since the invariant structures of the understanding with which he operates are essentially dynamic even in their isomorphic relation with the known, this does not lead him to build into his cognitional theory the rigid and static subjectivity that characterises the Kantian categorial structure of the understanding. It is the subjectivity of a voluntarist intentionality, more like the conative and pragmatic form which the stream of consiousness takes in the thought of William James.[13]

This voluntarist intentionality (*intentio intendens*) derives from what Lonergan calls the *self-affirmation* of the knower through which all scientific method is grounded in the rational interiority of the human subject in its drive to know being.[14] Here the self-affirmation which is latent in all human knowing like an immanent law is made explicit in the consciousness of the knowing subject as he reflects upon the dynamic structures inherent in his understanding and deliberately appropriates them as a set of directives to guide the process of his knowing heuristically to its goal. But that is possible as we have seen, only if the structures of our rational consciousness can anticipate the goal and only if the goal is isomorphic to those structures. This implies such a correlativity between knowing and being and being and knowing that Lonergan defines being as the objective of the pure desire to know.[15] Does this mean that all that we can know is being proportionate to the structure of our knowing, that we can never reach the objectively real? That might be the case if knowing were extrinsic to being itself, to being as being, if knowing were one thing and being another. But it is not like that, for the knower participates in being and is himself being, and his knowing grounded in his self-knowing is itself a form of being: hence the relation between knowing and being falls within being and presupposes the intrinsic intelligibility of being, and knowing is intrinsically oriented not only to being proportionate to knowing but to being as being, to the objectively real.[16]

Lonergan draws an important distinction here between proportionate being and transcendent being.[17] Proportionate being is being proportionate to our knowing, being which is not only understood and affirmed but is experienced by the human knower, being with a determinate structure proportionate to the determinate structure of our knowing. But properly the notion of being is an unrestricted notion, for being is not only all that is known but also all that remains to be known, and it is being in this full, unrestricted sense that we desire to know.[18] Thus, while being falls partly within our inner or outer experience, and partly beyond our inner and outer experience, transcending the bounds of all actual human experience, it does not fall outside the pure desire to know but is indeed its proper objective. Transcendent being, then, is being that extends indefinitely beyond all our cognitional acts, while penetrating and underpinning their conceptual contents, and is the core of their meaning. It is towards being in this transcendent sense that human knowing is ultimately headed, as is evident in the basic orientation of human knowledge beyond the known to the unknown or in man's unceasing questioning of his questions in an unrestricted desire to know. This implies a profound interior connection between the open, heuristic structures immanent and operative in our human knowing and the unrestricted, indeterminate content, the infinite openness of being itself. That is to say, it implies 'an immanent source of transcendence' in man, in virtue of which his knowing is not confined to the universe of proportionate being but goes beyond it to the realm of transcendent being.[19] While this is a feature underlying all human knowledge, it constitutes the structural root in man's understanding where he is open not only to the absolute transcendence of being as such, and therefore not merely to the idea of God as the unrestricted act of the understanding,[20] but to the absolute transcendence of God in his infinite *reality* over all created being. In other words, this 'immanent source of transcendence' in man constitutes 'the basic anthropological component' of Lonergan's method, but this needs to be matched with 'the specifically religious component', if we are to advance from transcendental method to theological method, from 'general transcendent knowledge' to 'special transcendent knowledge'.[21] Here the transcendental question as to God is not repudiated but is opened out beyond itself through the self-revelation of God, and correspondingly the self-affirmation of the human knower which plays such a key rôle in Lonergan's general transcendental method is not repudiated but yields to an intentional self-transcendence in which the religious subject seeks what is independent of himself in an unrestricted thrust of self-transcendence.[22] That is to say, the prior notions that constitute the very dynamism of our conscious intending, and as the upper heuristic blade of scientific method constitute the common core and ground of the methods of the particular sciences, remain in operation and hold good in the field of theological inquiry (as well as in every other field of inquiry). Thus they provide the normative pattern for the interpretation of religious experience, and as its active correlate they shape and unify that experience and mediate its content in the realm of meaning.

CONVERSION

In the transition from general transcendental method to specific theological method, however, a significant change takes place which Fr. Lonergan calls 'an about-face', for in religious experience we are concerned not simply with a heuristic intentionality directed beyond what we already know and experience but with the 'unknown' reality of God who in his love has taken the *initiative* in communicating himself to us.[23] That is the *prior* fact, 'the specifically religious component', with which we have to reckon in theological method, a religious experience that precedes knowledge, a dynamic state of affairs in which the human subject has already responded to the love of God poured out upon him through the Spirit, and in which the assent of faith has anticipated understanding.[24] This is the change that takes place in *religious conversion*. Conversion is an existential, intensely personal and utterly intimate experience in which a transformation of the subject and his world takes place, for in conversion he moves from one set of roots to another, and becomes a different self with a new understanding of himself which affects his understanding of everything else.[25] Lonergan speaks of religious conversion as 'other-worldly falling in love', the new beginning that takes place when God floods our hearts with his love and we on our part fall in love with God. By the gift of his love God has come to occupy the ground and root of our intentional consciousness at its highest level, and we love him with our whole heart and our whole soul and with all our mind and strength.[26] Thus being in love with God is the basic fulfilment of our conscious intentionality, in which our latent capacity for self-transcendence becomes an actuality.[27]

> Being in love with God, as experienced, is being in love in an unrestricted fashion. All love is self-surrender, but being in love with God is being in love without limits or qualifications or conditions or reservations. Just as unrestricted questioning is our capacity for self-transcendence, so being in love in an unrestricted fashion is the proper fulfilment of that capacity. That fulfilment is not the product of our knowledge and choice. On the contrary, it dismantles and abolishes the horizon in which our knowing and choosing went on and it sets up a new horizon in which the love of God will transvalue our values and the eyes of that love will transform our knowing.[28]

In this way religious conversion is 'thematised' and 'objectified' by Lonergan as 'a modality of self-transcendence' and is made to play an explicit rôle in a dynamic theological method.[29] Along with intellectual conversion and moral conversion which it presupposes, it involves 'an about-face and new beginning'. Intellectual conversion involves a radical shift from a way of knowing that is like 'looking at' things, with its corresponding notion of 'objectivity', to another way of knowings things as they are given in experience and mediated by true acts of meaning, for it is the world mediated by meaning which is the 'real world'.[30] Such an intellectual conversion in which we break free from often long-ingrained habits of thought and speech takes place only through a process of self-transcendence, that is the 'self-appropriation which is itself a grasp of transcendental method'.[31] Such a process involves a movement through four realms of meaning, which Lonergan speaks of in terms of common sense (description through relating things to onself), theory (explanation in terms of the inter-relations of things in themselves), interiority (the appropriation of one's rational self-consciousness as the source and ground of constitutive meaning), and transcendence. According to Lonergan, it is only when we advance beyond classical theology which distinguished only two realms of meaning, common sense and theory, and acknowledge interiority as a distinct realm of meaning that we can begin with a description of religious experience and acknowledge a dynamic state of being in love without restrictions.[32] In moral conversion there takes place a change in our principal motives or a change in the criterion of our decisions and choices, from satisfactions to values, that is, from decisions in terms of the advantage and disadvantage or the pleasures and pains involved to decisions in terms of objective values or transcendental precepts.[33] This is a process of moral self-transcendence into a state in which we are grasped by values beyond and independent of ourselves and a process of growing moral self-determination in which we attain freedom from bias and rationalisation. From an initial thrust towards moral self-transcendence constituted by the judgment of value itself as a transcendental notion we advance to the existential moment when we discover ourselves as moral beings in the realisation that in opting for value against satisfaction, when value and satisfaction conflict, we thereby make ourselves authentic human beings and indeed constitute ourselves as originators of value in ourselves and in our society.[34] In moral conversion, then, there takes place a movement from the self-transcending to the self as transcended in an intentional thrust toward unrestricted moral self-transcendence. The attainment of such unrestricted moral self-transcendence is only reached in religion when we fall in love with God, but apart from strict association of the love of God with self-transcendence, e.g. in the denial of the self to be transcended, it easily becomes misconstrued through erotic notions.[35]

Religious conversion advances beyond intellectual and moral conversion while taking them up into itself, for it introduces something new and distinct and puts everything on a new basis.

> Religious conversion is being grasped by ultimate concern. It is other-worldly falling in love. It is total and permanent self-surrender without conditions, qualifications, reservations. . . .
> As intellectual and moral conversion, so also religious con-

version is a modality of self-transcendence. Intellectual conversion is to truth attained by cognitional self-transcendence. Moral conversion is to values apprehended, affirmed, and realised by a real self-transcendence. Religious conversion is to a total being-in-love as the efficacious ground of all self-transcendence, whether in the pursuit of truth, or in the realisation of human values, or in the orientation man adopts to the universe, its ground and its goal.[36]

Religious conversion means more than a new and more efficacious ground for the pursuit of intellectual and moral ends, even though it corresponds to and fulfils the latent capacity and desire in the human spirit for self-transcendence: it has a distinct dimension of its own which does not derive from this world, but derives from the transcendent reality of God himself and his other-worldly love.[37] However, without the transcendental notions to which man's intentional self-transcendence gives rise, the transcendent itself is nothing in this world and the love of God remains an unknown mystery. Hence God's gift of love flooding our hearts is something we are unable to understand except on the vectorial basis of our rational interiority and within its realm of constitutive meanings, in which we relate experience of God's love to our cognitional and moral self-transcendence and interpret it in terms of their conscious operations and dynamic structures.[38]

KNOWLEDGE AND LOVE

Here we come to a really decisive point in Lonergan's theology, which he emphasises again and again by rejecting the principle, *Nihil amatum nisi praecognitum*, Knowledge precedes love.[39] Religion regarded as a dynamic state of being in love with God constitutes a realm in which *'love precedes knowledge'*, for *'who it is we love, is neither given nor as yet understood'*.[40] What is given in this experience is a quite new self and a new understanding of oneself, and thus a new basis from which the religious subject can advance toward knowledge. Latent in all this is an 'infused wisdom' which derives from the love or grace of God poured into our hearts by his Spirit — that is, the *lumen gratiae* or *lumen fidei* of the older manner of speech.[41] Faith is here identified with the state of being in love which is the human spirit's response to the love of God, but as such it is a form of love that precedes knowledge, and only advances to knowledge as we reflect upon it and allow it to come to expression within the world mediated by meaning. This does not mean that the gift of God's love is conditioned by human knowledge: rather is it the cause that leads man to seek knowledge of God, the source of the orientation in the human spirit toward the unknown or the transcendent. In other words, Fr. Lonergan identifies the infused light of grace or the infused light of faith with the structural root of transcendence in the human subject, which he regards as not only the ground of religion but the transcultural base upon which the world of meaning and therefore universal communication repose. It is through religious conversion, in the experience of being in love with God which fulfils our profound intentionality, that this inner connection comes to light. Hence the *precognitive* love or grace that floods our hearts through the Holy Spirit given to us could be the finding that grounds our seeking God through natural reason and through positive religion.[42] It is, however, by consciously relating the reality of God's love given in experience to the immanent orientation toward the transcendent in man and by reflecting on it in the real world mediated by meaning that *knowledge* of it develops through processes of understanding, judging and believing.[43]

This is the context in which Lonergan speaks of *the word*. In its most general sense it means 'any expression of religious meaning or religious value'. While its carrier may be intersubjectivity, in which meaning is embodied, or art or symbol, or remembered and portrayed in lives and deeds, it is normally in language, spoken and written, that the word is expressed.[44] This is, however, word in its external expression which Lonergan calls 'outer word' in contrast to the 'inner word' which is 'the speech of spirit within spirit' and which as such is prior to any use of language.[45] In the basic theological sense in which he uses the term, the word is the speech of love to love: *Cor ad cor loquitur*, word in its immediacy, prior to its expression in the world of meaning. The word of God, therefore, is 'the inner word that is God's gift of his love', 'the prior word God speaks to us by flooding our hearts with his love'.[46] While Lonergan can speak of the word of God as both 'an inner grace and the outer word that comes from Christ' and also speaks of that word, in virtue of its authoritative source, as 'doctrine',[47] it is clear that by the word of God he refers to the movement of the precognitive love of God in our hearts, that is, where God's 'speaking' is identical with 'flooding our hearts with his love'. This is a prior word which in its immediacy is non-cognitive and non-conceptual, for it does not pertain to the world mediated by meaning but to the unmediated experience of the mystery of love and awe, in which image and symbol, thought and word (in the usual sense) lose their relevance and even disappear.[48] This prior word which God 'speaks' to us by flooding our hearts with love Lonergan identifies with religion, but it is clearly word used in a figurative sense, but when he says that 'by its word, religion enters the world mediated by meaning and regulated by value', he is clearly using the term *word* in his other sense, as an expression of religious meaning or of religious value. In the strict sense, then, it would appear that the prior word in its immediacy only really becomes *word* when it finds expression in the world mediated by meaning and when it takes on the form of an outwardly spoken word. Lonergan insists, however, that such an outward word is not something incidental: on the contrary it has a constitutive rôle to play.[49] Hence he argues that when God pours out his love upon us, we are not concerned just with God's gift of his love.

> There is a personal entrance of God himself into history, a communication of God to his people, the advent of God's word into the world of religious expression. Such was the religion of Israel. Such has been Christianity. Then not only the inner word that is God's gift of his love but also the outer word of the religious tradition comes from God. God's gift of love is matched by his command to love unrestrictedly, with all one's heart and all one's soul and all one's mind and all one's strength.

Thus

> the word of religious expression is not just the objectification of the gift of God's love; in a privileged area it also is specific meaning, the word of God himself.[50]

By that Lonergan appears to mean that the word of religious expression is not just an historically conditioned expression of the love of God, whose meaning depends on the human context in which it is uttered, but as announced in the Gospel embodies the inner grace and outer word that comes from Christ, and as such provides the transcultural inner core or the permanent base out of which special theological categories and doctrines are derived.[51]

Thus, although the word of God in himself (*quoad se*) is identical with the gift of his love through the Holy Spirit, in the personal powerful speech of love to love which is antecedent to our knowledge, as his self-giving and self-revelation *to us* he lets it take a form toward us (*quoad nos*) in the field of our rational interiority where it comes to intelligible and communicable expression. It penetrates into the inner word of the human understanding where our understanding is always a speaking of the human spirit within itself, and where the inner word takes intelligible shapes within the cognitive structures of our understanding, and therefore as such it is the specifically religious component which complements and fulfils the basic anthropological component, the normative pattern of our conscious and intentional operations as religious subjects.[52] In that way the word of God enters the world of meaning and history with such power that it demands belief, and the belief which it actually evokes is an extension of the precognitive faith that is born of religious love.[53] In the nature of the case, however, beliefs arise and take shape within the world of meaning and history, and as such are socially and historically conditioned by the way in which God's self-revelation is received in contexts varying from place to place and from one generation to another.[54] Hence Fr. Lonergan draws a real distinction between faith and belief, faith being defined through its immediate correlation with the love of God flooding our hearts, and belief being defined through its correlation with the word of religion as it enters the world mediated by meaning and regulated by value. This is a distinction, he claims, which secures a basis for ecumenical encounter and for an encounter between all religions with a basis in religious experience, for while there are inevitably divergences in belief, behind them lies a deeper unity in the knowledge of faith born of religious love which is the true ground of belief.[55] It is this distinction which allows the transition from Augustinian symbolism to Thomist intellectualism, and the transition which Lonergan claims to carry through from a basis in theory to a basis in interiority, without any departure from the permanent substance of the faith.[56]

BACKGROUND TO LONERGAN

There are, I believe, serious difficulties in this position, but in order to grasp the issues at stake we must consider, as briefly as the subject-matter permits, the historical roots of Lonergan's thought.

Lonergan's claim to lay bare an invariant, *a priori* but dynamic structure in the operations of the human mind, which is central to his position, evidently derives from a reinterpretation of the Augustinian-Thomist idea that the human soul understands itself by itself and thereby comes to know God on the ground of an inherent likeness, notwithstanding all its unlikeness, to God. In the *De Trinitate*, St. Augustine had advanced the view that in the mind itself, even before it is a partaker of God (*antequam sit particeps dei*) the image of God is to be found, in virtue of which it is capable of God and can be a partaker of him, and explained it in terms of a psychological structure in the mind's remembering, understanding and loving itself, in which a trinity, not yet indeed God but an image of God, is to be discerned.[57] These views were elaborated in the context of a wide-ranging metaphysics of a Platonic type in which the following features may be noted: (a) Augustine's famous illumination theory of knowledge, according to which the human mind is held to have a direct vision (not through the senses) of eternal truths or the world of intelligible realities through an intellectual light continuously reflected into the understanding from God — he could speak of this light variously as the presence of God within the mind and as the mind's participation in the Word of God;[58] (b) An account of the intellect as both active and passive, according to which knowledge is held to be produced in us both from the knower and from the reality known (*ab utroque enim notitia paritur, a cognoscente et cognito*), for unless something of our own is subjoined to the incorporeal or intelligible realities we would not be able to employ them to regulate our judgments of corporeal realities;[59] (c) A doctrine of the inner word in terms of which what we know inwardly and at first formlessly through the shining of intellectual light takes symbolic form in the mind as word (*verbum*), which belongs to no specific language (*nullius gentis linguae*), but is the inner act of the mind by which it both understands itself and formulates its thought and which as such becomes the vehicle of meaning. This inner word is to be distinguished from the outer word and the reality meant, the sign and the thing signified, as an intermediary 'significate', the inwardly conceived mental event through which knowledge takes place, provided that it is a true word concerning a true thing (*verbum verum de re vera*).[60]

This was the teaching St. Thomas inherited from St. Augustine, but he recast it within an Aristotelian framework of metaphysics, with its characteristic emphasis upon sense experience and abstraction, which he proceeded to develop in his own way. He replaced the Augustinian vision of eternal truth with an ontology of knowledge in which the light of the human mind is regarded as a created participation in the uncreated light of the divine mind; and accepted and adapted Aristotle's doctrine of the agent and possible intellect in such a way that he was able to show that the intellect penetrates into things in order to grasp them from within, and knows them through an immanent object which it produces within the human understanding, an *emanatio intelligibilis*, which is the procession of the inner word. Lonergan describes this inner word as 'the self-expression of the self-possessed act of understanding'.[61] This bringing together of the agent intellect with a created intellectual light makes the intelligence very much an active principle, and thus the conception or procession of the inner word an active operation of the understanding. Thus Lonergan says:

> . . . intelligence in act does not follow laws imposed from without, but rather it is the ground of the intelligibility in act of law, it is constitutive and, as it were, creative of law; and the laws of intelligible procession of an inner word are not any particular laws but the general constituents of any law, precisely because of this naturalness of intelligibility to intelligence, precisely because intelligence is to any conceived law as cause is to effect.[62]

This is an interpretation of Aquinas that is admittedly *psychological*, in which the focus of attention is directed upon the inner experience and self-understanding of the human mind,[63] and in which the inner word emerges with an act of self-understanding as a medium between the understanding and the reality understood.[64] Here St. Thomas's debt to Augustinian interiority is fully acknowledged, but is given an *intellectualist* slant, in which emphasis passes beyond the conceptual acts of the intellect or understanding to what understanding *is*, i.e. to the inherent structure of the understanding

understanding itself.⁶⁵ 'The human soul understands itself by its understanding, which is its proper act, perfectly demonstrating its power and its nature', as St. Thomas says.⁶⁶

This is a point of capital importance for Lonergan. An Aristotelian doctrine of knowledge by identity and an Augustinian-Thomist doctrine of created participation in the uncreated light of God are brought together in such a way that the agent intellect is identified with the ground of intellectual light and is revealed to be itself the active principle of intellectual light in the understanding, and so an intrinsic relation is posited between the intelligence and the intelligible, in virtue of which the human understanding is able to transcend itself, passing beyond mere relativity to know immutable truth. Furthermore, in the understanding which understands itself through itself, i.e. by referring its intellectual light to its origin in uncreated light and by reflecting that intellectual light upon itself, there is disclosed an immanent structure which is claimed to have universal validity.⁶⁷ So far as general knowledge is concerned, this immanent structure of the understanding, in respect of its potency, form and act, supplies the all-important 'constant' which Lonergan claims to be the key to scientific knowledge for it is invariant to the changing content of theories.⁶⁸ So far as Christian theology is concerned, this structure of the understanding is correlated with a metaphysical psychology of the essence of the soul, its potency, habits and acts, which is complemented by an entitative concept of grace, the supernatural intermedium between God and the human understanding which takes the form of infused light or infused faith.⁶⁹ That is to say, by being poured into the structure of the understanding understanding itself, infused grace becomes linked with the inner word or 'the self-expression of the self-possessed act of the understanding', to constitute the *religious interiority*, the self-understanding of the religious subject which lies at the heart of theology.⁷⁰

LONERGAN'S REINTERPRETATION

Having appropriated this classical mediaeval tradition through a psychological and intellectualist reinterpretation of the thought of St. Thomas, Fr. Lonergan essays to transpose what he has learned into an essentially 'modern' mode of thought. Fundamental changes have taken place which 'modify man's image of himself in his world, his science and his conception of science, his history and his conception of history, his philosophy and his conception of philosophy'.[71] The two principal facts with which Lonergan seeks to come to terms are: the fact that science gives up any claim to necessity and truth, and settles for verifiable possibilities that offer an ever better approximation to the truth; and the fact that philosophy is impelled to migrate from the world of theory to find its basis in the world of interiority.[72] His answer is the development of a *method* in which we operate with 'interiorly differentiated consciousness', determining 'its basic terms and relations by adverting to our conscious operations and to the dynamic structure that relates them to one another'.[73] Thus conceived, as we have already seen, method is a normative pattern of operations with cumulative and progressive results. This involves, on the one hand, the discovery of inherent and invariant structures, norms and procedures of the human mind and their open-eyed use as the upper heuristic blade of scientific activity, and on the other hand, an appropriation and objectification by the human subject of his own interior consciousness, in order to effect the transposition of systematic meaning from a static to an ongoing, dynamic context. That is to say, behind all scientific method stands the active, inquiring human subject, with his polymorphic, differentiated consciousness, whose mind is constitutive of meaning.[74] That is how we are to understand religious experience, with its transcultural inner core, determined by God's gift of love and man's consent; and as distinct from its outer manifestation which is subject to variation, this is what provides the base out of which theological categories are derived.[75] This is a religious and theological application of the principle Lonergan laid down in *Insight*:

> Thoroughly understand what it is to understand and not only will you understand the broad lines of all there is to be understood but also you will possess a fixed base, an invariant pattern, opening up all further developments of understanding.[76]

SOME CRITICAL REFLECTIONS

Several lines of critical reflection upon these views may now be offered.

(1) A fundamental difficulty that runs through all Fr. Lonergan's thought is his failure to cope with the basic dualism of his

Augustinian-Thomist inheritance. This dualism which is both epistemological and cosmological, has its roots in the sharp distinction between the intelligible and the sensible, between God and the world, which lies behind St. Augustine's symbolist-aesthetic orientation in knowledge and his belief that in its search for the truth the mind must turn in upon itself, for it is in the depths of the self-understanding where it is illuminated by an uncreated light light from beyond that the truth is to be found. While Aristotelian-Thomist thought tries to overcome this dualism epistemologically by operating with the principle that there is nothing in the mind which was not first in the senses, it is at the expense of a harder distinction between an immutable, impassible God, the unmoved Mover, and the sensible, transient world of contingent existence. Lonergan's intellectualist reinterpretation of Thomist thought through distinguishing two sources of knowledge, an extrinsic origin on the level of sense, and an intrinsic origin in the light of our intellects'[77] had the effect of reinforcing psychological and religious interiority, while retaining the detached relation of immutability and impassibility between God and the world, making all the more necessary an intermediate realm of causal grace between them.[78] So far as our immediate discussion is concerned, the difficulty of Lonergan's position is very evident at three decisive points: (a) the notion of an intermediate word between the understanding and what it understands; (b) the notion of an intermediate word of God between what he is in himself and what he is in our human understanding of him; and (c) the notion of a static analogy of being between what the understanding is in the structure of its self-understanding and the mind of God in which it participates. The significance of the first two notions can be brought out by contrasting them with the teaching of St. Anselm. With Lonergan's Thomism, the intermediate word, an abstractively derived immanent intelligible object is grounded upon the self-constitutive nature of the human understanding, and as such imports a considerable shift from objective meaning to constitutive meaning, from the truth of being to intellectual truth, which stands in sharp contrast to St. Anselm's doctrine of the 'real word' (*verbum rei*), word objectively grounded in and determined by the reality it signifies, directing us to the truth of created being (*veritas essentiae rerum*) and beyond to the Supreme Truth, the source of all truth, truth of being and truth of statement.[79] With Lonergan's Thomism 'word' as applied to God is ultimately a 'notional' concept, for in God himself there is only undifferentiated Light or Intelligence, so that *intelligere* and *dicere* may not be distinguished in God.[80] With St. Anselm, however, *dicere* cannot be simply equated with *intelligere* in God, for 'word' as applied to God is a real concept, which Anselm calls *locutio apud summam substantiam*. That is to say, the Word as word is consubstantial with God, and exists as Word in God eternally, and as such is the creative source of all other 'word' or 'locution', such as the *locutio rerum,* the objective intelligibility of the truth of created being. The fault in Lonergan's position has a long history, the psychological definition of word deriving from Augustine, reinforced by Aquinas through his Aristotelian psychology, which cannot be applied as such to God, but behind all that lies the fault of a dualism, in which he is unable adequately to relate God's *being* to his *act*, what he *is* to what he *does*: Lonergan's God does not interact with our world by deed or word in such a way that his own immediate being is inherently active in his deed and his word. Lacking this kind of living interaction between God and the world, or a proper doctrine of the Holy Spirit, Lonergan has to operate with a *static* analogy of being between the invariant structure of the human self-understanding and its created participation in the intellectual substance of God, in which the *dynamism* is an attribute of the human mind rather than God who remains immutable and impassible. That is to say, a static analogy of being, grounded on what the human intellect *is,* gives rise to a powerful voluntarist intentionality and agent intellect or the active reason.

(2) These difficulties are considerably reinforced when Lonergan undertakes his great migration in thought from a mediaeval to a modern context, and so seeks to transpose his intellectualist reinterpretation of mediaeval science and theoretic interiority, to modern empirical science and modern rational self-consciousness, for the kind of science and the kind of philosophy which Lonergan appropriates both involve epistemological and cosmological dualism, and both operate, not unnaturally therefore, with a realm of intermediate representations (the phenomenalist 'ideas in the middle') between the human understanding and what it seeks to know. Here Lonergan's two sources of knowledge, the extrinsic and the intrinsic, fall apart in the widening gap between 'science' and 'philosophy' — that is, between a science that is concerned not with explanatory penetration into the interrelations of things or

therefore with intrinsic intelligibility but is concerned only with probable truth or therefore with hypothetical intelligibility, and a philosophy which is impelled by the advance of this kind of science to move behind the changing worlds constructed by scientific theory to find their basis in a world of interiority and the methodically constant structures of rational self-consciousness that lie behind and accompany all human inquiry. Thus, under a misguided view of modern science (concerned only with approximations to truth) and a misguided acceptance of post-Kantian critical philosophy (the phenomenalist attempt to ground all cognition on the data of consciousness), Lonergan tries to retract out of theoretic penetration into the objective structures of reality, and to retreat into the subjective structures of man's self-understanding, in the hope of finding 'certainty' in the permanent structure of 'method', when it is no longer possible to find it in the changing content of scientific theories. But all this depends, in the last analysis, upon an isomorphic relation between the structure of the understanding as it understands itself and the structure of scientific knowledge which gives rise to a concept of knowledge by identity. This is not a dynamic isomorphism, the correlation (of which Einstein speaks) that becomes manifest in the advance of scientific inquiry between the understandability (*Verständlichkeit*) of the universe independent of our conceiving of it and the structures of our scientific theories, for the *invariance* with which Lonergan works is inherent in the structures of the understanding apart from the material content of knowledge — i.e. Lonergan stands the Einsteinian concept of invariance on its head in which Einstein himself could only have regarded as impossibly subjectivist.[81]

This transposition from an Augustinian-Thomist intellectualist interiority into the critical interiority of modern historical self-consciousness has an astonishing effect upon Lonergan's theology: it makes it a first cousin if not an actual twin of Neo-Protestant *Glaubensverständnis* or *Glaubenslehre*, in which a reflection upon inward religious experience or the truths of the faith, abstracted from material conditions of space and time, replaces classical objective theology. This is particularly evident in a comparison with Schleiermacher who, in view of the widening gap between 'knowledge' and 'meaning' opened up by Newtonian observationist science and the 'Copernican revolution' of Kantian philosophy, shifted the centre of gravity from 'knowing' to 'understanding' (*Verstehen*), or from intelligibility to meaning. Here we have a distinction between thinking as a form of 'inward speech' and speech as an 'external form' of thinking, which closely parallels the teaching of Lonergan.[83] The understanding of both inner speech and outer expression is sought within a realm of meaning in which the inner connections between the historico-cultural self-consciousness of the religious community and the creative spontaneous activities and self-determinations of the human spirit are brought to light, not least in the inter-personal structure of human life and existence as 'the whole' within which communication takes place. Here too we have a stress upon the fact that the human spirit expresses its inward feeling and deepest insight in symbols and myths that follow the laws of image and affect rather than of logic,[84] and so here too theology does not derive from an objective word grounded in the being and activity of God as God in living interaction with the world he has created, but from reflection upon religious affections which derive from the love of God immanent in the religious consciousness through the indwelling of God's Spirit, and takes the form of religious expression in the Christian community.[85] Owing to a radical gap between the given and the not-given, Schleiermacher is forced to find a way across the gap by a philosophy of non-conceptual knowing by 'identity', an inner isomorphism between the human spirit and the divine Spirit, and thus offers a reinterpretation of the Incarnation of the Word of God in space and time in the conviction that God does not become anything.[86] On Schleiermacher's view the Word became not flesh but meaning. If David Tracy's interpretation is right this is very like Lonergan's position. For the divine revelation is primarily the entry of the Judaeo-Christian God not into the world of nature but into the world of meaning and history. Or it is, to employ *Insight*'s categories, an entry into the field of interiority as conscious finality towards being. And the key categories (because the key operations) in that movement are no longer immediately metaphysical ones (as with Aquinas) nor even those derived from scientific intelligibility (as in *Insight*) but rather those categories of constitutive meaning.[87] In view of all this, it is an enormous pity that Lonergan has apparently never studied the struggles of Karl Barth with post-Kantian thought, for that might have helped to prevent his neo-Catholic theology from collapsing into a form of neo-Protestant *Glaubensverständnis* that takes its basic cue from an anthropological starting-point.

(3) The reason, of course, why Lonergan stands so close to modern neo-Protestants is that he still stands with them within the dualist structures of eighteenth and nineteenth century science and philosophy, and has not undertaken the last and all-important horizon-shift to *post-analytical science* and *post-critical philosophy*. He is certainly not unacquainted with contemporary science and some of its most far-reaching epistemological insights, but he interprets them with the dualist structures they have left behind. That is evident not only in his misunderstanding of Einstein's concept of invariance, noted above, but in his strange and persistent insistence that modern science is concerned only with probability implies an operationalist and instrumentalist notion of science in which probability and objectivity conflict, and in which probability is confused with degree of confirmation. As Popper points out, however, modern science does not seek highly probable theories but *explanations* yielding increase in material content, and that explanatory power and high content are in inverse proportion to probability.[88] Thus, if Lonergan's view of science were valid it would be impossible to account for the enormous advance in actual scientific knowledge. Helpful as they have been, then, Lonergan's various analyses of the contrast between Aristotelian and 'modern' science reveal that he has not awakened to the immense revolution in the foundations of thought that has come to light with relativity theory, in which the old dualisms between structure and substance, form and being, and therefore between theoretic penetration into the inherent interrelations of things and 'understanding', have been left behind for a unitary and profoundly synthetic form of thought.[89] This is a way of thinking in which we are no longer concerned, as with Aristotle, Aquinas and Lonergan, with the primacy of *quid sit* but with the primacy of *quale sit*, that is with the kind of scientific question in which we allow the field we are investigating to disclose itself to us in accordance with its own nature and in the light of its own internal relations. It is unfortunate that Lonergan's constant but sadly mistaken attack upon intuitive apprehension (e.g. in Duns Scotus) as an extrinsecist 'looking at' has apparently blinded him to the real cues he could have found in mediaeval thought for the all-important horizon-shift needed today, that is, in the Anselm-Grosseteste-Duns Scotus rather than in the Abelard-Albert-Aquinas line of thought, for it is there that we find already deep in the Middle Ages modes of inquiry and apprehension in which know-

ledge of things in their objective and inner structure does not involve an abstraction between explaining and understanding and in which a theoretic grasp of things in their inner logic (*ratio veritatis*) involves a synthetic co-ordination of different levels of form and being open upward but not reducible downward, which clearly anticipates modern scientific knowledge. In theological science, however, this imports a method in which the theoretical and the empirical, form and content, structure and substance, and therefore method and subject-matter, are interfused from the start and are never allowed to be torn apart. It is this way of thinking in natural and in theological science alike, which forces us to put to Lonergan the question whether he has really been concerned with *scientific method* in knowledge or only with the rational-psychological processes accompanying knowing, and a knowing at that which is construed only within the old dualisms of a pre-Einsteinian world.

NOTES

1 *Method in Theology* 112.
2 *Ibid.* 2, cited from a remark of Sir David Ross about Aristotle.
3 *Ibid.* 4.
4 For this contrast between classical and modern science, see the chapter on 'Dimensions of Meaning', in *Collection* 252 ff.
5 *Method* 4.
6 *Insight* XVIII, XXVI, 103 f., 392, etc.
7 *Method* 13 f.
8 *Ibid.* 25.
9 It is to this that chapter 4 on 'Religion' is devoted, 101 ff. Cf. also chapters 19 and 20 of *Insight*.
10 *Insight* 399 f.; cf. 115, 484 f., 576, *Collection* 142 ff., and *Method* 21.
11 *Insight* 486. David Tracy, *The Achievement of Bernard Lonergan* 52, 60, 136 shows this to be an identity of the knower and the known.
12 *Insight* 332, 483 ff.
13 *Ibid.* 181 f.
14 *Ibid.* 319 ff.
15 *Ibid.* 348 ff.
16 *Ibid.* 499 ff., 552 ff. Cf. here, William E. Reiser, 'Lonergan's View on Theology: An Outline', *Scottish Journal of Theology* 25. 1, 1972, 7 f.
17 *Insight* 391 ff., 640 f., 652 f.
18 *Ibid.* 350 f.
19 *Ibid.* 634 ff.; *Method* 75 ff., 102 f.
20 *Insight* 684 ff.
21 *Method* 25, *Insight* 634 ff., 687 ff.
22 *Method* 104 ff., 109 ff.

23 *Ibid.* 118 f., 237 f.
24 *Ibid.* 112 f., 115 f., 122 f., 289 f.
25 *Ibid.* 130 f., 240 f., 267, 271.
26 *Ibid.* 107, 112 f., 122 f., 115, 240, 242.
27 *Ibid.* 105.
28 *Ibid.* 105 f., cf. 115 f.
29 *Ibid.* 131, 241, 270 f.
30 *Ibid.* 238 f.; see also ch. 2, 57 ff., 75 ff.
31 *Ibid.* 83, 95.
32 *Ibid.* 81 ff., 114, 120.
33 *Ibid.* 240; see ch. 2, 27 ff.; 34 ff., 40, 50, 121 f.; and *Insight* 601 ff.
34 *Method* 32, 38, 50, 242.
35 *Ibid.* 107 ff., 111, 121 ff.
36 *Ibid.* 240 f.
37 *Ibid.* 242.
38 *Ibid.* 110 f., 274 f.
39 *Ibid.* 122, 278, 283, 340.
40 *Ibid.* 122 f.
41 *Ibid.* 123.
42 *Ibid.* 282 ff., 340 f.
43 *Ibid.* 238.
44 *Ibid.* 112.
45 *Verbum, Word and Idea in Aquinas* X.
46 *Method* 112, 119.
47 *Ibid.* 298.
48 *Ibid.* 112.
49 *Ibid.* 112 f.
50 *Ibid.* 119.
51 *Ibid.* 112 f., 282 ff., 288 ff., 298.
52 *Ibid.* 115 f., 198 f.
53 See *Verbum*, especially ch. 5 on *Imago Dei* 184 ff.
54 *Method* 41 ff., 361 ff.; see further chs. 12 and 13.
55 *Ibid.* 115 f., 118 f., 123.
56 *Ibid.* 276.
57 *De Trin.* XIV. 8. 11.
58 *Ibid.* XII. 15. 24, etc.
59 *Ibid.* IX. 12. 18; XII. 2. 2; cf. VIII. 3. 4.
60 *Ibid.* IX. 3. 3; 7. 12-11. 16; XIV. 7. 10; XV. 12. 21-23; cf. *Verbum* X-XIII.
61 *Verbum* 42, 82.
62 *Ibid.* 34.
63 *Ibid.* IX, 38 ff., 45 f., 63 ff., 76 ff., 217.
64 *Ibid.* 228 f., 192 f.
65 *Ibid.* 75 ff., 142, 151 ff., 184 ff., 210 ff., 218 f.
66 *Summa theologiae* I q.88 a 2 ad 3m. See *Collection* 149.
67 *Verbum* 79 ff., 85 ff., 89 f., 197 ff.
68 *Collection* 150 f.
69 *Method* 288 f.
70 *Ibid.* 246 f., 270 f., 282 ff., 285 f., 289 ff., 320 ff.

71 *Ibid.* 317.
72 *Ibid.* 259, 274 ff., 304.
73 *Ibid.* 274.
74 *Ibid.*, 246, 253, 262 ff., 270 f., 290, 302 ff.
75 *Ibid.* 281-293.
76 *Insight* XXVIII.
77 See *Verbum* 81 ff.
78 Cf. here, *Grace and Freedom*.
79 Cf. here 'The Place of Word and Truth in Theological Inquiry according to St. Anselm', *Studia mediaevalia et mariologica,* edit. by R. Zavalloni, Rome, 1971, 133-160.
80 *Verbum* 191 ff.; see 'Scientific Hermeneutics according to St. Thomas Aquinas', JTS, new series, vol. XIII. 2, 1962, 259-290.
81 See *Collection* 145 f., and *Insight* XXV ff., etc.
82 See *Collection* 121 ff., and *Method* 350.
83 See 'Hermeneutics according to F. D. E. Schleiermacher', SJT, 21. 3, 1968, 257-267.
84 Cf. Lonergan's references to Vico in this respect, *Collection* 262 f., *Method* 73, 205, 229.
85 *Method* 59 ff., 76 ff., 110 ff., 118 ff., 240 ff., 272 ff., 281 ff., 296 ff., 311 f., 347 ff., 361 ff.
86 Cf. here Peter Lombard's notorious dictum: *Deus non factus est aliquid!*
87 Op. cit. 207 f.
88 Karl Popper, *Conjectures and Refutations* 57 f., 218 ff.
89 Cf. A. R. Peacocke, *Science and the Christian Experiment,* 1971, ch. 2.

Method and Cultural Discontinuity

Nicholas Lash

CULTURAL DISCONTINUITY

It is now nearly a decade since Lonergan warned us that the contemporary cultural crisis — more specifically, the 'breakdown of classical culture'[1] — was imposing 'mountainous tasks' upon, was inviting 'to Herculean labours', 'Catholic philosophy and Catholic theology' (loc. cit.). *Method in Theology* is the mature fruit of Lonergan's attempt, over many years, to respond to this daunting challenge. The very first paragraph indicates that it is precisely the replacement of the 'classicist notion of culture' (culture as 'one . . . universal and permanent') by the 'empirical notion of culture' as 'the set of meanings and value that informs a way of life' (p. xi), which renders some such analysis of method necessary for the fruitful development of theology in our time.

Lonergan, therefore, undoubtedly takes very seriously the problem of cultural mutability, in general, and that profound, all-embracing mutation which Western culture is currently undergoing, in particular. Indeed, one of the most reliable of his interpreters regards the examination of 'certain key historical figures or periods in which a horizon-shift has taken place'[2] as a recurring indication of this characteristic concern. Nevertheless, the aim of this essay is to argue that the value of *Method* is significantly reduced by a failure to come to grips with the problem of *discontinuity* between different 'ways of life' (whether successive or contemporary), and thus between the 'sets of meanings and values that inform' them. Carefully to attend to shifts of culture, language, 'horizon' or 'epistemé', is not necessarily to treat with sufficient seriousness the problems generated by the discontinuities between different cultural contexts.

It could be objected immediately that, even if it were shown that Lonergan has failed to come to grips with such problems, the value of *Method* would not be significantly reduced, because the degree of attention paid to problems of cultural discontinuity is only a matter of emphasis. Such an objection rests on the assumption that these problems, however urgent and intractable, are not the heart of the matter where issues of method, interpretation and human understanding are concerned. This assumption I believe to be mistaken. There is impressive, cumulative evidence, from a wide range of academic disciplines, that such problems *are* at the heart of the matter, and that any exercise in methodology which marginalises them is guilty of a serious diagnostic failure. (Nor is this a merely academic issue, in the narrow sense, as any student of social, racial, class or cultural conflict and incomprehension would surely agree.)

In order to keep this essay within manageable limits, I shall restrict myself to an examination and critique of the relevant passages in *Method*. The disadvantage of this procedure is that it rules out the possibility of providing any of that evidence to which reference was made in the previous paragraph.[3] However, the texture of *Method* is so closely woven as to make it more or less impossible, in a single essay, both to enter into critical dialogue with Lonergan himself and to expose the background against which the critique is mounted.

There are four features of *Method* which I propose to discuss from the standpoint of the problem of cultural discontinuity: Lonergan's claim that method yields 'cumulative and progressive results' (p. 4); his appeal to the transcultural invariance of transcendental method; his treatment of community; and the place which the functional specialty 'communications' occupies in his schema. Since each of these features of the book is also discussed by other contributors to this collection, from other points of view, a certain amount of overlapping is inevitable.

CUMULATIVE AND PROGRESSIVE

The 'preliminary notion of method' offered by Lonergan is that of 'a normative pattern of recurrent and related operations yielding cumulative and progressive results' (p. 5). Although this preliminary notion is specified, fleshed out, qualified, as the argument proceeds, it continues to exercise a dominant and pervasive influence throughout the book.

Is this notion a preliminary description of the method which has, in fact, more or less explicitly characterized the process of theological enquiry, discussion and debate during two thousand years of Christian history? Or is it a description of the method which has characterized 'good' or 'successful' theology in the past (and, if this is the claim that is being made, what are the grounds on which the value-judgement is based?) Or is it a recommendation as to the method which *should* characterize theological operations in an 'empirical' culture such as our own (and, if so, what are the grounds on which this prescription is made?)

The first of these possibilities cannot be sustained. According to Lonergan, 'Results are progressive only if there is a sustained succession of discoveries; they are cumulative only if there is effected a synthesis of each new insight with all previous, valid insights' (p. 6). In different cultural contexts, at different periods, countless Christian theologians have had insights which, at least in some particulars, could appropriately be described as 'new' and 'valid'. But when has any theologian, or school of theology, been rash enough to claim that this or that new insight has been effectively synthesized with '*all*' previous, valid insights'. Or, were such a preposterous claim to be made, how could it be cashed? Where are the historical or hermeneutical tools which could render possible the substantiation of such a claim?

The suggestion that the results yielded by the intellectual operations of Christian theologians during two millenia could, as a totality or even in respect of their central axis, appropriately be described as 'cumulative and progressive' would seem to rest on the assumption that theological history is appropriately described in terms of 'evolution' or 'progress'. Lonergan has for many years been far too conscious of the phenomena of cultural 'bias' and 'decline' to fall into this trap.[4] Nevertheless, there are indications that, where the scientific dimension of theological understanding is concerned, evolutionary assumptions play a larger part in Lonergan's thought than is consistent with a full recognition of the hermeneutical problems posed by the fact of significant discontinuity between different cultural epochs and contexts. Thus, for example, his discussion of 'the historicity of dogmas' (pp. 324-326) still seems to appeal to a notion of the cumulativity of dogmatic history which has been rendered problematic by recent developments in historiography. But this very fact suggests that, if the first of the three possible interpretations, outlined above, of the preliminary notion of method is untenable, it may be worthwhile briefly to consider the second.

In the chapter devoted to 'systematics', Lonergan lists 'four factors [that] make for continuity' (p. 351) in theology. One of these is 'the occurrence in the past of genuine achievement' (p. 352). It is not difficult to admit that there have been, in every area of enquiry and discovery, 'genuine achievements of the human spirit' such that, unless their 'substance is incorporated in subsequent work, the subsequent work will be a substantially poorer affair' (*loc. cit.*). But this admission leaves unanswered precisely those questions concerning the criteria for recognizing such achievements, and the possibility of their successful 'incorporation' into significantly different social, cultural and linguistic contexts, which are central to contemporary hermeneutical debate. And until these questions *are* answered, such 'genuine achievements' as have occurred in the past constitute a purely potential, and not an effective, or actual, 'factor making for continuity'. Because the argument of *Method* is conducted, throughout, at a high level of formal and heuristic abstraction, the impression is given, again and again, that Lonergan is unduly confident that the tasks set by his formally pure prescriptions can, in fact, be successfully executed.

Where specifically theological 'achievements' are concerned, there is a further difficulty. We are told that 'To put method in theology is to conceive theology as a set of related and recurrent operations cumulatively advancing towards an ideal goal' (p. 125). For Lonergan, 'Christian theology' is 'conceived as *die Wendung zur Idee*, the shift towards system, occurring within Christianity' (p. 144). The 'ideal goal' is that of 'the total view or some approximation to it' (p. 128), a 'comprehensive viewpoint' (p. 129), 'the perfection of complete immobility' (p. 138). It is, indeed, true that Lonergan regards this ideal as unattainable within history. And I would wish to endorse his lifelong insistence that the human quest for strictly theoretical understanding and explanation has an appropriate and necessary place in Christian theology. But what sort of concepts of the mystery of God, of revelation, of faith, of sanctity and suffering, lie behind an *expression* of that insistence in terms such as those which I have just quoted?

Such questions lie outside the scope of this essay, but it may be worth offering the suggestion that Lonergan's concern to vindicate the role of theoretical understanding in theology has led him to misconceive the nature of that 'cognitive interest' [5] which specifically characterizes the dynamic structure of *fides quaerens intellectum*. Lonergan does not conceive of theological method on the analogy of method in the natural sciences,[6] but he does claim that, methodologically, theology and natural science have certain common features, in virtue of their common grounding in 'transcendental method'. These common features are most clearly discernible in the realm of strictly theoretical (or explanatory) discourse, but it may be that, for all its indispensability, this realm is not that at which Christian theology most fundamentally and characteristically operates. Nor is it adequate to suggest, as Lonergan does, that the other realms in which Christian theology operates are exhaustively classified as the realms of 'common sense', 'interiority' and 'transcendence' (cf. pp. 81-85). One of the weakest features of *Method*, as another contribution to this collection suggests, is the inadequacy of its implied concept of revelation. Yet it is only critical reflection on Christian revelation which can appropriately determine the characteristically Christian 'realms of meaning' or 'cognitive interests'. And it may well be that the common features shared by theological and literary method (the latter, for Lonergan, is — significantly — merely a form of 'common sense': cf. p. 72) are at least as significant as are those shared by theological method and method in the natural sciences.

Be that as it may, it is sufficient for my purpose to point out that it is possible to admit the occurrence of 'genuine achievements' in theology without conceiving of theology as 'advancing', during the course of its history, towards some 'ideal goal' of total explanation. Lonergan's tendency to regard the achievements of 'successful' or 'good' theology in these terms is at least partly due to that inattention to problems of transcultural understanding and interpretation which is the focus of my concern in this essay. To see why this should be so, it is necessary to turn to his chapters on 'History' and 'History and Historians'.

Lonergan's description of critical history (cf. pp. 190-192) appeals implicitly to his conception of method as cumulative and progressive. He claims that 'there exist procedures that, *caeteris paribus,* lead to historical *knowledge*' (p. 196, my stress). This claim, and the arguments which he adduces in support of it, indicate a healthy reaction against that total historical agnosticism, or relativism, which characterizes some contemporary historiographical writing. He is aware of 'the problems of historical relativism . . . [of] the influence exerted on historical writing by the historian's views on possibility, by his value-judgements, by his *Weltanschauung*' (p. 195), and so on, but he omits discussion of these problems on the grounds that they are 'brought under control, not by the techniques of critical history, but by the techniques of our fourth specialty, dialectic' (*loc. cit.*).

In the following chapter, we begin to suspect that this postponement of the problem is inadequately grounded. We are told that the reason why 'history is rewritten for each new generation' is simply the 'incomplete and approximate character of historical narrative' (p. 215). Again: 'The past is fixed and its intelligible structures are unequivocal. . . . It is incomplete and approximate knowledge of the past that gives rise to perspectivism' (p. 220). In view of these remarks, it is not surprising that the problem of reconciling conflicting interpretations of history is, once again, postponed to the chapter on dialectic (cf. p. 224).

Among the distinctive features of the treatment of 'dialectic' are its individualism and its moralism. 'Not all opposition is dialectical. There are differences that will be eliminated by uncovering fresh data. There are the differences we have named perspectival, and they merely witness to the complexity of historical reality' (p. 235). But, as we have already seen, these latter differences are simply due to 'incomplete and approximate knowledge of the past'. In other words, if — *per impossibile* — historians knew 'all about' the past (and what could that *mean*?), the only conflicts that remained would be those 'stemming from an explicit or implicit cognitional theory, an ethical stance, a religious outlook', and these 'are to be overcome only through an intellectual, moral, religious conversion' (*loc. cit.*). Lonergan thus gives the impression that there is some one, single, correct understanding of the past, which may be asymptotically approached in the measure that historians accumulate 'correct' results by increasing the range of their information and eliminating subjective differences through 'conversion'. There is an air of profound unreality about this moralistic (and ultimately, positivistic) view of historical disagreement, and we shall return to the topic in later sections of this essay.

The individualism of Lonergan's treatment becomes explicit in the claim that 'perspectivism results from the individuality of the historian' (p. 246). I suggest that, if we are to do justice to those aspects of Lonergan's argument which we have so far considered, it is necessary to recognize that, for all the talk of social process and 'ongoing collaboration', he is primarily interested in improving the quality of the performance of the individual practitioner in each of the theological specialties. In other words, the third of the possibilities listed at the beginning of this section is that which most closely corresponds to the intention underlying Lonergan's formulation of his 'preliminary notion' of theological method. And it is possible that this over-riding preoccupation with improving the quality of the performance of the individual academic specialist largely accounts for what I earlier referred to as the marginalisation of crucial problems generated by the element of discontinuity, and incommensurability, between different social, cultural and linguistic meaning-contexts.

In order to test this hypothesis, we need to examine the rôle played by the analysis of community in the overall argument of *Method*. Before doing so, we shall turn to another area in which the individualism of his concern is apparent: namely, his treatment of the transcultural validity of 'transcendental method'.

TRANSCENDENTAL METHOD

Reference has already been made to 'the occurrence in the past of genuine achievement' as one of the four factors which Lonergan sees as making for theological continuity. These factors seem to be listed by him in order of methodological importance. If this is so, then it is significant that the first two should be 'the normative structure of our conscious and intentional acts' (p. 351), and 'God's gift of his love . . . [which] is ever the same love, and so it ever tends in the same direction' (p. 352). As making for continuity, these two factors are closely interrelated. Lonergan is well aware that the normative structure of our conscious and intentional acts may be, and frequently is, violated. Fundamentally, it is his trust in the abiding gift of God's love as creative and redemptive presence in man's pilgrimage which makes him confident that, in the long run, the necessary 'conversions' will occur, restoring or enhancing the authenticity of our conscious and intentional acts.[7]

A case can be made out for the suggestion that the fundamental metaphysical options which all men take (whether explicitly or not) may be rational, even though they are not capable of being *theoretically* justified.[8] Therefore, the central rôle played by trust in divine providence in the thought of men such as Lonergan (or Newman, whose cast of mind is strikingly similar at this point) does not automatically justify charges of fideism or irrationality. Such charges would, however, have a certain plausibility if the appeal to the normative structure of our conscious and intentional acts, *as* a factor making for continuity, rested solely on trust in the abiding gift of God's love, and lacked any autonomy and empirical testability. Lonergan is aware of this. His appeal to the normative structure of our conscious and intentional acts, as a factor making for continuity, is grounded, not only in his trust in divine providence, but also in his conviction that the dynamic structure of human intelligence is, in its fundamental features, transculturally invariant. This observation is of considerable importance. In order to explore it in rather more detail, it is necessary to turn to the section on the derivation of the categories in the chapter on 'foundations'.

In that section, we are told that 'the transcendental method outlined in our first chapter is, in a sense, transcultural' (p. 282), and that, 'Similarly, God's gift of his love (Rom. 5, 5) has a transcultural aspect' (*loc. cit.*). Therefore, 'There exist . . . bases from which might be derived both general and special categories that in some measure are transcultural' (p. 283). Not the least interesting feature of these remarks is their unusually *tentative* nature: 'in a sense'; 'aspect'; 'in some measure'. This note of hesitation is, perhaps, the nearest that Lonergan gets to acknowledging the force of those problems with which this essay is concerned. In *what* sense is transcendental method transcultural? In *what* measure may transculturally applicable categories be derived? In order to answer these questions, a further question is necessary: what are the 'bases' from which the categories are derived? Lonergan's answer is clear, and it is unlikely to surprise anyone familiar with the development of his thought: 'The base of general theological categories is the attending, inquiring, reflecting, deliberating subject. . . . The subject in question is not any general or abstract or theoretical subject; it is in each case the particular theologian that happens to be doing theology' (pp. 285-286). In other words, the empirical basis for the affirmation that 'the transcendental method . . . is, in a sense, transcultural', is the fundamentally invariant dynamic structure of the intellect of individual human beings, of every age, class and culture.

That this is the case is already made clear in the first chapter, that on 'method'. In this chapter, distinguishing between 'categorial' and 'transcendental' modes of intending, Lonergan allows that the former may 'vary with cultural variations', but he contends that the latter are 'invariant over cultural change' (p. 11). The transcendental modes are 'experiencing, understanding, judging and deciding' (p. 14). But is not the pattern of transcendental method possibly subject to significant variation or revision? No, the dynamic structure which is expressed in that pattern 'is not open to radical revision. . . . [Because it] is the condition of the possibility of any revision' (p. xii). 'Obviously, revision can affect nothing but objectifications. It cannot change the dynamic structure of human consciousness' (p. 19). The dominance of Lonergan's concern with the structure and performance of the individual thinker, which we noticed in the previous section, enables him to slip in that 'Obviously', and so to evade some of the awkward questions which a less individualistic centre of attention would have forced him to treat with greater seriousness. Therefore he is able to assert that 'There is . . . a rock on which one can build' (p. 19), and that 'The rock . . . is the subject' (p. 20).

Now, it must indeed be admitted that Lonergan's insistence on the fundamentally non-revisable and culturally invariant cognitional structure of the human subject is of more than trivial significance. Were it not the case that we are entitled to trust in this, our persistent attempts to understand would have no rational basis. If there were no common constituent features shared by the cognitional structure and performance of all those whom we recognize as human subjects, our classification of those subjects *as* human would be meaningless. As Wittgenstein said, if a lion spoke, we should not understand him.

Nevertheless there do seem to be, from the point of view of method, two serious weaknesses in Lonergan's analysis. In the first place, precisely because transcendental method *is* transcendental, and not categorial, it tells us nothing about *how* particular individuals, members of particular societies, go about the business of attending, inquiring, judging and deciding. Transcendental method, as purely formal, is of little assistance to us as we seek to understand, to interpret, to transpose propositions from one (alien) meaning-context to another (our own).

In the second place, as a result of his preoccupation with the invariance of transcendental method in individual subjects of all ages, classes and cultures, Lonergan pays comparatively little attention to the bewilderingly wide range of methods of cognitional procedure which characterize different social and cultural contexts. In order to understand the individual, we must understand the concrete cultural context of which he is a constituent element. It is not too obvious that, where the concrete work of interpretation, understanding and transposition is concerned, the individual subject *does* constitute a rock on which we may successfully build.

It could be objected, however, that I am overemphasizing the individualism and formality of Lonergan's treatment. After all, there is a great deal in *Method* about community, culture, and incarnate meaning. To these aspects of the book we must now therefore turn.

MEANING AND COMMUNITY

Lonergan is at pains to insist that 'there exist quite distinct carriers or embodiments of meaning' (p. 64), and his account of 'incarnate meaning' is a fuller description of that 'empirical notion of culture' which we quoted at the beginning of this essay: 'Incarnate meaning combines all or at least many of the other carriers of meaning. It can be at once intersubjective, artistic, symbolic, linguistic. It is the meaning of a person [or group], of his way of life, of his words, or of his deeds. It may be his meaning for just one other person, or for a small group, or for a whole national, or social, or cultural, or religious tradition' (p. 73).

Problems of interpretation arise because commonsense expressions have 'intersubjective, artistic, symbolic components' that may appear strange in a social and cultural context other than that which generated them (cf. p. 154). Lonergan therefore admits that 'we are aware of the great differences that separate present from past cultures' (*loc. cit.*). Interpretation aims at bringing us 'to an understanding of the common sense of another place, time, culture, and cast of mind. This is, however, the enormous labor of becoming a scholar' (p. 160). That conclusion is, once again, significantly individualistic. It simplifies the task of interpretation by failing to draw attention to the fact that the interpreter's success depends not only upon his scholarly skills, but also upon the extent to which he himself, in heart, experience and head, shares the whole range of those 'distinct carriers or embodiments of meaning' which characterize his own culture or way of life. Not infrequently, the professional interpreter's world of appropriated meaning is so restricted that he is accused, not without justice, by his contemporaries of living in an academic ivory tower.

If Lonergan had placed more emphasis on the extent to which the scholarly interpreter himself embodies that range of distinct carriers of meaning which characterize his own class, culture, world, or 'way of life', the problem of interpreting an alien context would have been shown to be more profound, and intractable, then it appears to be from the pages of *Method*. This becomes clear if we turn to the section on 'functions of meaning' (pp. 76-81), or to the two earlier essays to which Lonergan there refers us.[9]

'Social institutions and human cultures have meanings as intrinsic components', and such institutions (and, therefore, surely, the meanings which they embody), 'can be subjected to revolutionary change' (p. 78). Community, Lonergan insists in a splendid passage which is worth quoting in full, 'is an achievement of common meaning, and there are kinds and degrees of achievement. Common meaning is potential when there is a common field of experience, and to withdraw from that common field is to get out of touch. Common meaning is formal when there is common understanding, and one withdraws from that common understanding by misunderstanding, by incomprehension, by mutual incomprehension. Common meaning is actual inasmuch as there are common judgements, areas in which all affirm and deny in the same manner; and one withdraws from that common judgement when one disagrees, when one considers true what others hold false and false what they think true. Common meaning is realized by decisions and choices, especially by permanent dedication, in the love that makes families, in the loyalty that makes states, in the faith that makes religions. Community coheres or divides, begins or ends, just where the common field of experience, common understanding, common judgement, common commitments begin and end' (p. 79; cf. *Collection*, p. 245, the differences are trivial). 'Meaning enters into the very fabric of human living but varies from place to place and from one age to another' (p. 81). Not the least important feature of this analysis of community as an achievement of common meaning is its grounding of common meaning in common experience. Those problems of discontinuity between different (successive or contemporary) cultural contexts, with which this essay is concerned, arise in no small measure from the extent to which the field of common experience shared by the inhabitants of two different cultural contexts is often so minimal, so overshadowed by the areas of experience which they do *not* share, as to render them mutually unintelligible. Lonergan comes close to recognizing this when he speaks, towards the end of the chapter, of the 'homogeneity necessary for mutual comprehension' (p. 99).

Why is it that, in spite of his lucid and penetrating analysis of human community as an achievement of common meaning, recognition of that heterogeneity which obtains between so many successive or contemporary cultural contexts has so little influence on the structure and argument of *Method*? The answer is partly to be sought, I believe, in that preoccupation with the formal, theoretical dimension of theological discourse to which we have already drawn attention. But although a case could be made out for the claim that the 'language' of, for instance, pure mathematics is more or less transculturally invariant (and even this claim would not, I suspect, go unchallenged amongst contemporary experts in logic and linguistics), Lonergan surely overestimates the extent to which the strictly theoretical dimension of theological discourse is purely formal (or explanatory) and, as such, more readily available than are the 'commonsense' carriers and embodiments of Christian meaning? Without in any way denying (to repeat the reassurance) the importance of the distinction between 'commonsense' and 'theoretical' discourse, is this distinction quite as *sharp*, where Christian theology is concerned, as Lonergan would have us believe? Earlier in this essay, I suggested the possibility that the common features shared by theological and literary method are at least as significant as are those shared by theological method and method in the natural sciences. And, as Lonergan notes, whereas 'the technical treatise aims at conforming to the laws of logic and the precepts of method, literary language tends to float somewhere in between logic and symbol' (p. 72). As such, it is more closely dependent upon the other constituents of whatever cluster of meaning-contexts it is an element, than a purely formal language would be.

Another reason, I suspect, why the discontinuities of meaning between experientially heterogenous contexts do not constitute a problem which receives close and sustained attention in *Method* is that the entire process from data to ultimate results, of which the eight functional specialties represent distinct and separable stages, is concerned with 'working out the suitable transposition from one culture to another' (p. 150). The discontinuity between that world of meaning whose expressions constitute, in any given situation, the data for mediated theology, and that world of meaning in which the results of the process are to be communicated, is not sharply felt, in *Method*, because the process from data to results is, as it were, presented as a mediating structure between the two. Therefore, in our final section, we shall make some observations concerning the place which the functional specialty 'communications' occupies in Lonergan's schema.

COMMUNICATIONS

Tracy faithfully expounds Lonergan's thought when he insists that 'the question of communication emerges as a properly theological question only after each of the first seven functional specialties has played its proper rôle. For no more than intuitionist theories can save the epistemological day, can leaps from Jesus to the fabled man in the street save theology.'[10] As Charles Davis pointed out several years ago, in an essay strongly influenced by *Insight*, the 'danger of irrelevance' for theology today arises not from speculation, but from repeated attempts to communicate the fruits of biblical and historical research (the 'first phase' of *Method*) without first shouldering the burden of rigorous and sustained intellectual reflection: 'We must ask real questions, questions that cannot be met without fresh theological thought.'[11]

Nevertheless, even when this point is taken, and even when we remember that, in the architecture of *Method*, the functional specialty 'communications' also 'remains a strictly *theoretical* discipline',[12] strategically directing the collaboration of theology with the entire range of the human sciences, Lonergan's treatment and location of this specialty remains unsatisfactory. The grounds of my dissatisfaction are partly linguistic, partly ecclesiological, even partly sociopolitical.

In the chapter introducing the functional specialties, Lonergan says that 'Communications is concerned with theology in its *external relations*' (p. 132, my stress). The image of 'external relations' is ambiguous. It could (and does) refer to the relationship between theology and other human sciences. As such, it is unexceptionable. But it could (and does) also refer to the relationships between academic theologians and the rest of the believing community. Here, the use of the image is highly questionable.

To 'communications' falls the task of making 'the transpositions that theological thought has to develop if religion is to retain its identity and yet at the same time find access into the minds and hearts of men of all cultures and classes' (pp. 132-133). At this point, the suspicion begins to dawn that far too large a part of the contemporary theological enterprise has been shuffled off into a specialty the operations of which are to be found, for example, in the five volumes of Arnold's *Handbuch der Pastoraltheologie* (cf. p. 355). Moreover, the logic of the passage just quoted seems to suggest that the work of making the necessary transpositions falls exclusively to the eighth specialty. In that case, to what world of discourse does the language of the fifth, sixth and seventh specialties belong?

I have said that the grounds of my dissatisfaction with Lonergan's treatment of 'communications' are partly linguistic. For several decades, philosophers have been teaching us to be very wary of that model of the relationship between thought and language which may be crudely expressed in the form: first I have (non-linguistic) thoughts; then I put them into language. Is there not a social analogue of this model which, at least where the human sciences (including theology) are concerned, is equally misleading? What languages could it be in which the Christian fact is articulated in 'foundations', 'doctrines', and 'systematics', if not in languages which spring from the minds and hearts of people inhabiting determinate cultural contexts? Undoubtedly, the language of scientific theology needs to be as rigorous, and precise, as are the technical languages of other correlative academic disciplines. But what could it mean to suggest (if this is what Lonergan is suggesting) that reflection on the first phase finds its *initial* direct (mediating) expression in a world of discourse inhabited only by academic theologians? Is he perhaps assuming that the language of the fifth, sixth and seventh specialties is transculturally invariant? If so, then what are the grounds of this assumption?

To suppose that fundamental questions concerning the possibility of, and the criteria for, making the necessary transcultural linguistic transpositions can be postponed to the eighth stage of the process 'from data to results' looks like sleight-of-hand. Life would, indeed, be easier if the operations proper to the other specialties in the second phase could be carried out *before* these questions have been tackled. But this is simply not possible.

The same tendency illegitimately to postpone these problems can be detected in Lonergan's treatment of theological pluralism — the importance of which he acknowledges. According to him, the manifold differentiations of consciousness ground 'a multiplicity of the theologies that express the same faith' (p. 271). But is it, in fact, a genuinely *theological* pluralism that he is acknowledging? 'Primarily,' he says, 'that radical pluralism' in religious language 'that has its root in the differentiations of human consciousness' is 'a pluralism of communications rather than of doctrines' (p. 276). Or, as he puts it elsewhere, 'these many modes of speech involve no more than a pluralism of communications' (p. 329).

In the course of some recapitulatory remarks on meaning, ontology and community, Lonergan says that 'The genesis of common meaning is an ongoing process of communication, of people coming to share the same cognitive, constitutive, and effective meanings' (p. 357). Splendid, but it is not clear how this description of the genesis of shade meaning in the Church relates to that model of Christian meaning which sees theology as being concerned only in the eighth specialty with its 'external relations' with the rest of the Church. This difficulty indicates the ecclesiological ground of my disquiet.

Lonergan is far too sophisticated a thinker, and too competent a historian of theology, to be satisfied with any crude distinction between *ecclesia docens* and *ecclesia discens*. One fundamental weakness of this distinction was always its assumption that there were those in the Church who 'knew', whose business it was to communicate with those who did not. Communication was conceived as a one-way process, in which the body of the Church exercised a largely passive function. Is there not, in the implied relationship, in *Method*, between the practitioners of the eight specialties, and the rest of the believing community, a similar assumption, which is similarly inadequate as a description of the way in which the truth of Christ lives, and finds expression and embodiment, in the believing community? 'To communicate the Christian message is to lead another to share in one's cognitive, constitutive, effective meaning. Those, then, that would communicate the cognitive meaning of the message, first of all, must know it' (p. 362). But how do they *come* to know it? By their expert familiarity with the objects of the eight functional specialties, or by their participation in that collaborative effort of shared learning which constitutes the Christian Church,[18] and *within* which the work of academic theology is grounded and situated?

The ecclesiological weakness or, at least, ambiguity, that one detects in this final chapter of *Method* is but the theological expression of a cultural and political stance which I find equally unsatisfactory. 'The Church can become a fully conscious process of self-constitution only when theology unites itself with all other relevant branches of human studies' (p. 364). This, surely, is a programme of genuine collaboration, of two-way communication. But once again, apparently, only amongst the experts. Lonergan draws an analogy between the function of communications in theology and 'the execution of the plans' (p. 365) in society at large. But who are the 'planners'? Is the whole sociopolitical community engaged in this task (enlisting, of course, the total range of different skills enjoyed by members of that community), or must the community as a whole stand by, ready to execute the plans drawn up for it by a privileged minority? The suspicion that motivates this question is not dispelled by Lonergan's recognition that 'Execution generates feedback' (p. 366). Nor is it dispelled by the view of 'integrated studies' bringing 'theologians into close contact with experts in very many different fields. It will bring scientists and scholars into close contact with policy makers and planners and, through them with clerical and lay workers engaged in applying solutions to the problems' (p. 367).

CONCLUSION

I have learnt too much from Bernard Lonergan, over many years, not to be profoundly respectful of the sheer power and scale of his achievement in *Method in Theology*. But uncritical acceptance would be a strange way of expressing one's gratitude to one who has always laid so much emphasis on the indispensability of personal, critical reflection.

My contention in this essay has been that, for a number of reasons, not the least important of which are his preoccupation with the performance of the individual theologian, and his concern for the strictly theoretical realm of theological discourse, Lonergan has dangerously marginalised certain problems, generated by the element of discontinuity between different cultural contexts, which are currently central to theology's problematic. In the previous section, I did not more than hint at certain ecclesiological and sociopolitical assumptions which, I believe, facilitated this marginalisation. All aspects of theological enquiry and reflection are fully caught up in our contemporary cultural sea-change. Problems of intercontextual, intercultural, understanding and transposition have become increasingly important for all the human sciences. An analysis of theological method which does not treat these problems as methodologically central is doubly suspect: it is suspect both as to the possibility of its practical implementation, and as to the adequacy of its theoretical basis.

NOTES

1 Bernard Lonergan, 'Dimensions of Meaning', *Collection* (London, 1967) 266.
2 David Tracy, *The Achievement of Bernard Lonergan* (New York, 1970) 10.
3 Among recent studies which could be regarded as at least 'straws in the wind', see Michel Foucault, *The Archeology of Knowledge*, trans. A. M. Sheridan Smith (London, 1972); Imre Lakatos and Alan Musgrave, eds., *Criticism and the Growth of Knowledge* (Cambridge, 1970); Rodney Needham, *Belief, Language, and Experience* (Oxford, 1972); Bryan S. Wilson, ed., *Rationality* (Oxford, 1970). I have tried to suggest some of the implications for theology of contemporary shifts in historical experience and understanding, in Nicholas Lash, *Change in Focus* (London, 1973).
4 Cf. Bernard Lonergan, *Insight* (London, 1957) 218-242; *Method in Theology* 52-55.
5 Cf. Jurgen Habermas, *Knowledge and Human Interests*, trans. J. J. Shapiro (London, 1972).
6 Cf. his rebuttal of Langdon Gilkey in 'Bernard Lonergan Responds', *Foundations of Theology*, ed. P. McShane (Dublin, 1971) 224-225.
7 This section of the chapter on 'systematics' should be read in the light of the sections of *Insight* on the 'heuristic structure of the solution' to the problem of evil, pages which are in fact, though not explicitly, a sketch of fundamental soteriological and ecclesiological principles: cf. *Insight* 696-703, 718-730.
8 Cf. Anders Jeffner, *The Study of Religious Language* (London, 1972) 105-131.
9 Lonergan, '*Existenz* and *Aggiornamento*', 'Dimensions of Meaning', *Collection* 240-267.
10 Tracy, *op. cit.* 257.
11 Charles Davis, 'The Danger of Irrelevance', *The Study of Theology* (London, 1962) 26.
12 Tracy, *loc. cit.*

Divine Revelation and Lonergan's Transcendental Method in Theology

J. P. Mackey

I wish to offer here some reflections on the work of Bernard Lonergan. My hope is that they will form themselves into some systematic pattern and perhaps even point to some concluding insights concerning the present crisis in Christian theology. They are the reflections of one who is not a Lonergan disciple, not even a catechumen, but who has spent some time recently studying the Lonergan phenomenon; one whose main interest lies elsewhere, mainly with the theologians of hope, but who still could not ignore the enthusiasm of Lonergan's many disciples, the prestigious Lonergan congresses, and the almost apocalyptic tone of the expectation which awaited his latest book. These reflections are based on a reading of that book, *Method in Theology*, just published, on gleanings from an international seminar held on some pre-publication copies of that work at Maynooth, Ireland, in March of this year, and on some other publications of and about Lonergan, mainly his monumental *Insight*. The reflections are in part an apologia for my preference for some of the theologians of hope — those with most respect for the radical historicity of man's world — over transcendentalists of the Lonergan kind, and they centre loosely on the concept of divine revelation.

I should like to offer, first, some introductory remarks on the usage of the key words 'revelation' and 'transcendent'. I follow a usage of the word 'revelation' inherited from my tradition, a usage which distinguishes between the general revelation of God in nature and the special revelation of the same God in some historical events or persons of the past. At this point, for the sake of introductory brevity, I simply borrow a note from the history of religious to the effect that the particular divinity (or conception of divinity) which can be considered revealed in nature or cosmos (already-ordered-universe) has a name and a place and date of birth. His name is, or was, Logos. He was conceived at that period of Graeco-Roman civilization which witnessed intercourse between the late Stoic/Middle Platonist theology and the creation motif of the

Judaeo-Christian tradition. At birth he was seen to be a divinity who created this empirical world out of nothing and whose immutable mind contained the plan or law which would guide the world through all stages and vicissitudes to his final goal. He was, of course, of the male sex and he was generally reputed, by Christians, naturally, to have become Christian at the incarnation. Around the time of the Arian heresy he achieved undisputed lordship of the West. He was by definition a revealed divinity, since his mind could be read, partially at least, from the structure of the cosmos and its pilgrim's progress. He is but recently deceased. He served the empire well, and his passing has left a great emptiness in the Western soul. May his Father (cf. Philo) have mercy on his nous.

This Logos conception of divinity naturally facilitated and affected the particular use of the concept of revelation which Christian theology applied to those events it called special divine revelations. However, in nostalgic memory of a past order, I shall be concerned in the first half of this paper with the kind of transcendentalism which a revelation of God in the empirical world permits; and in the second half I shall take up the question of special revelation.

THE LAST OF THE CLASSICAL TRANSCENDENTALISTS?

The word 'transcendent', together with its derivations, is a word which can mean so many things that by now when it stands alone, it probably conveys no definite meaning at all, and consequently it would need to be paraphrased every time it is used. As linguistic currency it has been drastically devalued in contemporary theology. In the first hundred pages of Lonergan's latest book, for instance, the word is used of a method, an exigence, a process (self-transcendence, which even God can do, on p. 116) and a person (God is 'someone transcendent' on p. 109). By this stage the word has become a poor alibi for lack of precision in a man's thought. Again for the sake of brevity, let us say that the word 'transcendent' can express two quite different directions of thought, one classical, and the other much more contemporary.

The word 'transcendent' can clearly refer to truth. I mean both speculative and practical truth — to use another old distinction —

a norm for behaviour or a normative method, as well as some knowledge about the nature or structure of something, for instance. On the classical understanding of it, transcendent truth refers to propositions the meaning of which does not change in the course of history. According to a more contemporary direction of thought, transcendent truth could only refer to some creative insight by which, for now, I go beyond my present condition of existence, by which I go from one historical position to another, by which I take my part in the making of history.

The word transcendent can just as clearly apply to a process, to self-transcendence, for instance. Once again, the classical understanding of this process would require the existence or the present availability of transcendent truth, in the classical sense indicated above. The process itself would then be the gradual appropriation of this already-existing truth from clues afforded by cosmos in stages, and its end or goal would be knowledge-union with the Logos. Once again, a more contemporary understanding of this process would not require the existence or present availability of transcendent truth in the classical sense. It is possible for some living things to proceed to higher stages without it being necessary that any living thing, either extra- or intra-mundane, have already had in mind that which will actually be the higher and perhaps the highest stages of the future. To the obvious question: how does one then know one is going higher, making progress? (see the Platonic-Augustinian Fourth Way of Aquinas), one can only answer out of one's sense of continuity-change in this historical existence. One can perceive, at least in outline, a brief period of the evolution of successive life-forms and one can institute comparisons. One is aware of the manner in which human ideals, in either received or constructed forms, change even as human endeavour approaches their realization. One think of the way in which an evolution-theorist like Huxley or Teilhard de Chardin regards the cultural tradition factor as the great accelerating agent in the evolution process. It will be necessary to return to this theme of the radical historicity of existence in this empirical world.

The reference of the word 'transcendent' to persons, the phrase 'transcendent person', demands similar distinctions. For Sartre, at the end of his essay on Existentialism and Humanism, the human person is transcendent simply because it is the human condition to have to go out beyond oneself in order to truly ex-sist. This is the kind of living transcendence which Camus has in mind when, towards the end of *The Rebel*, he talks about the artistic creativity of man. In neither case is the dead transcendence of the already existing creator plan either necessary or welcome. The classical transcendentalist may, of course, mean no more than these when he talks about transcendent persons. It is, however, a fact of theological living that the phrase 'transcendent person' too often functions in the not-formally-introduced-as-such rôle of synonym for the classical divinity of the West; and as such it has played no small part — though by no means an honourable one — in the kind of reasoning to the existence of God typified in Lonergan's *Insight*.

If a transcendental method is one that allows me to transcend myself until I reach a stage of being or of contact with being, a goal which can obviously be called transcendent — after the method and the process — and if the transcendent can be used as a synonym for God (called 'a transcendent someone', as if personhood were any less analogically predicated of God than any other attribute), then I seem to have demonstrated God's existence. However, what has really happened is that a vacillating distribution of a middle term has cloaked a fatal inconsequence of logic.

In the remainder of the first part of this paper, then, I shall simply try to document my suspicion that Lonergan is a transcendentalist of the classical type, that his transcendental method could work only during the reign of the classical transcendent God of the West, the self-revealing Logos, and that both method and divinity are now either obsolete or obsolescent.

In order to suspect the presence of the direction of thought characteristic of the classical transcendentalist, one need only consider the following quotation from *Insight* (p. 676):

> If the real is being, the real is the objective of an unrestricted desire to understand correctly; to be such an objective, the real has to be completely intelligible, for what is not intelligible is not the objective of a desire to understand, and what is not completely intelligible is the objective, not of an unrestricted desire to understand correctly, but of such desire judiciously blended with an obscurantist refusal to understand.

The heart of this argument is the demand for total intelligibility, the demand that there *be* total intelligibility now, even if it is not presently available to any man. The source of this argument is that platonic concept of divinity as total truth, immutable exemplar plan for this universe, potentially intelligible to a (transcendentally) methodical mind working from the admittedly imperfect material of intra-mundane experience. The main concession which Lonergan makes to modernity is his acceptance of evolution and even of the random factor involved in it. But notice his curious claim: 'what is probable, sooner or later occurs' (I, 122). Even randomness is seen to be statistically regulated to the point of predictability in principle (the much higher randomness of human freedom is never given proper attention in this argument) and a divine truth or plan can still survive immutable from the beginning, only to be verified evolutionarily in the empirical world, though admittedly the plan is no longer as readily available to human inspection as it was in the static world of the Greeks. Whitehead too, who said that all Western philosophy was a series of footnotes to Plato, could rejoice in being himself a further footnote for all the process in his metaphysic.

Of course the empirical universe sets us problems of source and origin. But suppose we were to answer in terms of some unintelligible (to us) act of creation out of nothing, we still would not be able to decide if this empirical universe reflected, or was somehow (equally unintelligibly) governed by, an existing plan to a determined goal. At least we could not decide this independently of our groping researches in our universe here and now and, more importantly, of our partially free decisions on what to do in and with our universe, decisions which become more powerfully relevant to the future as our mental and technological power expands.

An old philosophy teacher of mine — who was a strict Thomist and never mentioned Bonhoeffer — used to say that, in a very real sense, God made no difference to this world. We cannot be said to know God. Our experience of contingency, which we extrapolate to our empirical universe, can be for us an incipient entrusting of ourselves to some indefinable ground of being. That entrusting perhaps makes our world seem more kin to us, more hopeful (is that the same as saying 'more intelligible'?), but after that it raises more questions than it answers. Is there some plan which is working itself out in our universe at the sub-human level? Think of the suspicion of teleology amongst the practitioners of the biological sciences, or the debate about orthogenesis between some followers of Teilhard de Chardin and other evolution specialists. And even if we commit ourselves to the view that God meant us to arrive on the scene (a further acknowledgment the content of which is not intelligible to us, at least as yet), how can we harmonize the real and growing creativity, or destructiveness, of our own freedom with any transcendental truth or plan of the classical kind? We do not know, nor can it be predicted even in principle, what our future or the future of our world will be, since that depends too much on what we make of it in our own free creativity. So we cannot say that being is completely intelligible. It is partially intelligible now and will be intelligible, presumably, in different ways in the future, because it will be made different. With God, too, though we have a certain access to acknowledgment of him, and though our partial understanding of patterns of evolution may give some hint of some initial plan in matter, it is much more a question of what he will be to us when we will be whatever we make ourselves, indeed *if* he will be to us; it is much more a matter of hope than of knowledge or affirmation of truth. In fact, the question of the existence of God and the problem of who or what God might be are inseparable, as philosophers who have argued against 'proofs' of God's existence, from Kant to Anthony Flew, have clearly seen. These problems are as inseparable as faith (commitment/acknowledgment) is from hope. Faith, love (*eros*, striving) and hope form one seamless robe.

How can I conclude with certainty that God is, as I presume to do at the end of a 'proof of God's existence', unless I can then say who or what he is, with at least some known degree of verisimilitude? Those who try to draw proofs of God's existence from the works of Aquinas would need to notice that when it comes to naming God, Aquinas, in what I believe to be his better moments, can declare himself the greatest agnostic of them all. No, we do not know who or what God is, and we do not know either, therefore, how far our feeble predications are from the truth of God. So, we cannot be said to know that God is, as we know that things on our level of knowing are. Our sense of contingency can be our acknowledgment of divinity. But, though that word 'acknowledgment' contains in itself the word 'knowledge', it is psychic activity of quite a unique kind. It could be described briefly, though by no means adequately, as a mixture of speculation and hope which leaves neither of these in pure form and which is only maintained in existence by struggle (*eros* or love). To say I believe in God (or that God is), I hope in God (or that God is), I love God (or love God to be), are different partial ways of saying the same thing. Our minds being so piecemeal as they are, there is probably no single adequate way of saying it. Or one might say that God belongs at least as much to the future as he does to the past or present, and the future does not exist; at least not yet. We do not *know* what it will be or even that it will be. We struggle towards it — because there is no option — in a mixture of speculation and hope. The speculation is based on the form of life we know. The hope is based on the speculation and generated by the struggle. That is also the profile of man's approach to God.

If we can go on and on and make things better; indeed, if we can just go on and on, this experienced power or spirit (as in Old Testament usage) will be our indication that God is and is with us, and it can even generate hope that we may meet God more directly, 'face to face' in an as yet unknown, because unbuilt, future. But by the very nature of our evolutionary-historical existence, which is our perennial access to acknowledgment/hope of God, there is no definitive truth or plan of God, or of our world which is now even in principle available to us. The intelligibility of being is in the *making* almost as much as, if not much more than, it is a given. And, from our point of view at least (and that is the only point of view we can adopt), it is in complete historical jeopardy.

We can be grateful to Lonergan for the manner in which *Insight* revised our too common notion that knowing is a matter of having ideas and images of objects. His emphasis on judgment and decision, on interiorization and self-appropriation, is of lasting value. But unless his understanding of the human spirit in the world has changed radically, in a manner not adequately indicated by his published works, his treatment of human cognitive activity is still too rationalist, too platonic. The very concept of a transcendental method which can be normative and critical (presumably in the technical philosophic sense of the word), though it appears fully-fledged only in his later work, is possible only in the context of a classical transcendentalism, the transcendentalism of the type of philosophy one finds in *Insight*.

A normative *and* critical transcendental method — as opposed to a piece of transcendental good advice, like 'do good and avoid evil' in the practical sphere, which, however normative it might be, cannot function as a criterion of good and evil since it achieves its transcendental status at the cost of being a purely formal precept or imperative — is only admissible if there is a transcendental truth, in the classical sense, which is partially or in principle available now to man.

That means, if there is in the mind of God a truth or plan for reality which is partially or incipiently visible in our empirical world, and which our empirical world successively expresses, but in no way alters by its own random elements or creative forces; if such a plan or truth could be said to exist in the mind of God, and if providence were the practical application of this eternal truth to this empirical world, then our empirical world would be all of a piece. There would be no real discontinuities, though many might appear in the present state of our knowledge merely because of its present imperfection. Then a divine plan, presumably consistent throughout and presumably immutable from eternity, would stretch from the moment of the creation of matter, over the long haul of the evolution process, to the very structure of the human spirit (which a Cartesian God would have made as his end product, naturally so that it really did or could know things as they really are), and it would await only final completion in the future. *Then* it would make sense to envisage a research method which would be first truly transcendental in the classical sense, that is, applicable though not confined to all the different fields of human study and all the categories of human understanding, second, normative in all these areas, and third, critical in the technical philosophical sense of that word, that is capable in itself of critically establishing truth or falsehood of matters arising in these areas (MT 20). Then also, especially at a time in the affairs of men when 'the sciences' are reporting all the most impressive advances, it would be tempting to look to these for the clearest illustration of such a method-in-practice. As Lonergan wrote in *Insight*: 'The precise nature of the act of understanding is to be seen most clearly in mathematical examples. The dynamic content in which understanding occurs can be studied to best advantage in an investigation of scientific methods' (p. x, see also p. xxiv, or simply note the structural sequence of *Insight*).

Such transcendental method postulates transcendental truth of the classical kind. But the Logos divinity of the Greeks is dead.

His obituary is recorded in the death-of-God movement — not of nineteenth century Europe, whose thinkers merely immanentized him, but of late twentieth century America. The One God of even the best religious thinkers of Platonism, however, is alive and well, we believe, and he beckons us towards the dark future.

Since the main interest in Lonergan at this moment focusses its spotlight on his thought about method, it is only right to look more closely at what he himself has to say about transcendental method. But before doing this, and indeed in order to do it more adequately, it is necessary to consider his views on special divine revelation. This is not a subject to which he himself has devoted much specific attention in either of the major works under consideration here. Nevertheless, some reference to what we may at least infer are his views on special revelation is necessary for at least two reasons. First, as Charles Davis indicated in his contribution to the 1970 Lonergan Congress (see Davis's article in FT), in reference to a subject other than revelation, if a method leaves relatively untouched a subject which with less consciously methodical people is undergoing important theological change, then one must suspect either the writer on method has not tried it out on concrete subjects or that its use makes little difference to them. Either way, that man's published method suffers seriously in its image. Second, and perhaps more pertinently, special divine revelation is often tacitly assumed to be a source of truth which is transcendental in the classical meaning of the word. Hence, some remarks on this subject are relevant to a discussion of transcendentalism in general and to transcendental method in particular.

REVELATION AND TRANSCENDENCE

Let us look first at Lonergan himself and then at some of his critics. It is not easy, to say the least, to decide how Lonergan now thinks about revelation, as many of his critics are quick to point out. The topic of revelation, at least in the sense of what has become known as the special revelation of God in history (as opposed to his general revelation in nature), was not of major concern in *Insight*, except in so far as Lonergan attempted a Blondelian apologetic in order to persuade us of the reasonableness of accepting a divinely revealed solution to a problem — the problem of evil — which had finally defeated the best efforts of our unaided reasons, and yet refused to go away. In *Insight* Lonergan talks about human belief in general as if it consisted of assent to propositions (p. 711), and he gives us no reason to think that he could define it otherwise when it occurs in the religious sphere, as man's assent to a divine initiative. Is this the so-called propositional view of revelation, and does he continue to hold this view right through his latest book on method?

Certainly there are sections of *Method in Theology* where the propositional view of revelation is strongly suggested — the view, namely, that truths were imparted to men by God, complete in conceptual category and verbal formulation. He writes:

> The divine initiative is not just creation. It is not just God's gift of his love. There is a personal entrance of God himself into history, a communication of God to his people, the advent of God's word into the world of religious expression. Such was the religion of Israel. Such has been Christianity. (MT 119)

Should we take 'God's word' literally here, as the propositional view of revelation would tempt us to do, as the Christian theology of Incarnation would suggest?

In another place, when he is dealing with the functional specialty of doctrines, Lonergan distinguishes the doctrines of the 'original message', the 'divine revelation in which God has spoken to us', from doctrines about these doctrines, from church doctrines, theological doctrines, methodological doctrines, and so on (MT 295-8). In a question in a section on development of doctrine, the question, namely, 'How is it that mortal man can develop what he would not know unless God had revealed it?' (MT 302), there seems to be implied a conviction that special divine revelation resulted in a deposit of truths already complete and inalterable in meaning-content. Development seems to have to do with the different forms in which the human mind can assimilate and express such revealed mysteries, the symbolic form, for instance, followed by the philosophic and then the systematic. Although the permanence of dogma is a function both of the fact that the mysteries are revealed and that the revealed meaning is infallibly declared by the Church, there can be progress in the understanding of this meaning (MT 323). This very point that there can be progress in understanding the meaning of revealed mysteries simply confirms the impression that special revelation results in a deposit of truths complete in formulated meaning — and how formulated, if not in words or equivalent symbol? — which men can progressively understand. Again, how can I progressively understand some meaning unless it be finally encapsulated in some formula of the past? If it is not so encapsulated, I really develop or change the meaning itself, I do not simply makes progress in understanding it.

Finally, *Method in Theology* also talks of belief as taking someone's word for something (p. 43), and declares that belief has the same structure in religion as it has in the general conduct of human affairs, where it is omnipresent, except that, in the religious sphere, it rests on a basis of faith (MT 118-9). If we leave aside for a moment this implied distinction between belief and faith, which suggests another avenue of access to God, other than through his special propositional (or equivalently formulated) revelation, since we shall have to consider that other one immediately, it can surely be said that the collection of contexts just presented does indeed convey a concept of special revelation as a deposit of truths with definitively formulated meaning, whether formulated in words or in equivalent symbols. And this is as close to the propositional view of revelation as anyone, after a decade at least of theological debate on the subject, would now care to come.

Yet, as phrases about a religious form of human belief which rests on a basis of faith would suggest, there is another line in Lonergan's thought which makes it highly doubtful that he is holding to a propositional view of revelation. When he writes about a prior word of God which pertains to the unmediated experience of the mystery of love and awe (MT 112), he is clearly not thinking of propositional revelation at all. He is clearly thinking, rather, of the grace, the spirit, the love of God which is poured into men's hearts to enable them to believe. In such contexts he seems perfectly satisfied that this prior act or 'word' of God is the fundamental source of man's religious faith. That there is no other access to God which could substitute for this or replace it is clear from his (new?) view in *Method in Theology* about reasoning to God's existence: questions about God's existence and nature, he is now convinced, are questions of the lover who seeks to know God better or the 'unbeliever' who seeks to escape him (MT 116). Demonstration of God's existence *à la* Vatican I finds its proper place in a state of pure nature (MT 339), now no longer with us.

So man's religion, man's faith, in such contexts is predicated totally on God's prior action in man's spirit, an action described as the inpouring of love, grace, spirit. In that foundational reality of the functional specialties which Lonergan calls conversion, the normal hierarchy is this: intellectual conversion (to the correct method, and the correct use of the correct method, and the correct results of the correct use of the correct method?) is normally the fruit of moral and religious conversion; moral conversion is normally the fruit of religious conversion; and religious conversion is always the fruit of God's grace (MT 267-8). Further, conversion, presumably occurring according to this normal hierarchy, can affect performance in other functional specialties besides that of foundations, to which it is central. It can affect the interpretation of past instruments which one offers, the history one writes, the place in dialectic which one occupies; it helps discriminate where dialectic has deployed the options and so it leads to the formulation of true doctrines (MT 161, 243, 270, 298). The rest is more mechanical.

Faith, then, 'is the knowledge born of religious love' (MT 115), of this experienced love of God poured into our hearts and of the love which is our graced response. That knowledge presumably finds expression in the words or alternate symbols which men find themselves able to create and use according to their time and place. 'The outwardly spoken word is historically conditioned: its meaning depends upon the human context in which it is uttered, and such contexts vary from place to place and from one generation to another' (MT 112). Here is variation in meaning, not just development in understanding of one and the same meaning, whatever in human experience that latter could mean.

Two sets of contexts; two different impressions. The impression from one set of contexts is of words or doctrines or truths which came from God with final formulated meaning, and these must obviously form the data with which theology works as it moves through its functional specialties from data to results. (But then must not one be converted to do research too, for how can one appropriate revealed truths except by faith? Yet Lonergan never admits specifically that conversion affects research, the first functional specialty.) The impression from another set of contexts is of some initiating act of God which men experience and draw into the universe of formulated meaning in accord with the changing conditions of place and time. (Here also, one will presumably need to experience some at least conative conversion to religious faith in order to appropriate its data; but the questions now will be: are data from the past necessary at all in this schema of things, cannot God's grace strike equally at any time or place, is any room left for transcendent truth of the classical kind?)

Are these two sets of contexts, these two impressions, contradictory or complementary? Is the language of the first just a concrete way of stating the substance of the second? One might argue that complementarity is more probable from Lonergan's talk about religious belief resting on a basis of faith, belief having to do with revealed truths and the faith on which it rests having reference to God's inner gift of grace. One could adduce Lonergan's plea for more integration of the treatment of natural and supernatural (the distinction between these, he feels, was finally drawn by Philip the Chancellor in 1230 A.D.), except that the distinction probably does not coincide in Lonergan's mind with the distinction of contexts outlined above. In the end, one can only say that Lonergan is not clear on this, and turn to his critics.

LONERGAN AND HIS CRITICS

In the two Lonergan congresses with which I am familiar, one through publication of its papers and one by participation, two different kinds of common criticism emerged. There were other individual criticisms and appreciations, of course, but these seemed to echo in a number of minds, however different the expression they may have found in words.

In the Florida congress of 1970 a number of critics worried about the rôle and place of conversion in Lonergan's theological method. In particular, they worried if the functional specialties which schematically preceded foundations, that is, research, interpretation, history and dialectic, could be called theology at all in the proper sense of the word, since, without reference to conversion their practitioners might not have to do with God or religious faith at all, but merely with recovery and development of some of its dead monuments. It is probable, however, that this kind of criticism need not touch Lonergan very closely, particularly after publication of *Method in Theology*. He is so often prepared to see the functional specialties change priority and place in the sequence, and so change the direction of mutual influence; he is so prepared to see conversion in particular influence schematically 'earlier' specialties in the sequence; that both he and his defenders can do a great deal to save him from this line of criticism. A price that has to be paid for this salvage operation, of course, is a more topsy-turvey picture of the doing of theology, which fits a little uncomfortably with the expectations of a man opening a book on method. Such a man expects to find a series of operations described to him clearly, together with the sequence in which they are to be used if he is to gain adequate and accurate results, and there is no doubt that a good deal of Lonergan's talk encourages this hopeless expectation. In practice, of course, the experienced theologian is quite used to allowing his subject matter and the circumstances of his operation to dictate to him his choice and arrangement of functional specialties; he is quite used, even, to performing some specialized methodical operations as part of his overall task which could be performed just as well by an atheist, and the resulting untidiness does not bother him in the least. Like every other craftsman he knows that order is fashioned as much as, if not more than, it is discovered in the semi-chaos of his world, and the fashioning, when it occurs, often tells him more about the concrete and complex method he used than he could ever say about method before any particular task is undertaken.

The only point at which Lonergan seems vulnerable to this first line of criticism is in his treatment of the first functional specialty, research, and then only to the extent that he fails to apply *specifically* to this first stage what he freely admits of other preliminary stages, namely, that conversion has an influence on the search for the truth in these areas. An avid disciple of his, however, could argue that the admission is there implicitly in the talk about mutual influence of functional specialties; he could allow some dissatisfaction, but save the honour of his master. This first line of criticism, then, only becomes serious for Lonergan in so far as it takes a different course and broadens out into the second kind of common criticism against him, this time at the Irish seminar.

If there is doubt about the rôle of conversion in the first functional specialty, called research, it is perhaps because there is confusion in Lonergan's own work about the nature of the data for theological reflection. Do these data consist in formulated truths deposited by special divine revelation at some point in the past, so that research is a purely historical (scientific, objective, etc., etc.; all the prestige adjectives) method for making them available for contemporary assimilation; or do the data consist in some experienced initiative of God, to which man's response must be conversion or refusal of conversion (in which refusal man understands what he is invited to and refuses), some experienced divine initiative which finds its own expressed forms, different at different times, so that research in documents of the past qualifies (and perhaps critically) the understanding of the data, but does not entirely supply them? Torrance wanted to know if Lonergan was an old-style Roman Catholic or a new-style Tillich, and he felt that Lonergan's work would not allow him to decide. This sentiment was echoed by many in different words.

The question which might strike the unbiased observer at the Maynooth seminar, however, is this: could anyone there, of Roman Catholic or other Christian denomination, resolve that problem any better than Lonergan did or could? It is a simple and inescapable fact of theology that people who use revelation as a primary category, people who start with, or live with, the conviction that God revealed former mysteries, must sooner or later admit that they deal in truth or truths which are the gift of God rather than the discovery of man. They may decide, as much modern theology of revelation has done, that such truths did not come either by a literal *locutio Dei* or by divine deposition of concepts or symbols in the inner minds of prophets; they may decide that these came somehow in historical events. But in that case they must see to it that the events in question are quite unique on the human historical scene, so that their divine origin and message is clearly decipherable, or that there are some specially illumined people around to read an otherwise undecipherable divine message from them. In either case the process of revelation is not complete until men are in possession of a structured message, a formulated divine meaning. Once that is the case, we late-comers are dealing with truth or meaning which can be quarried in history but not changed by history; we are dealing with transcendental truth in the classical style.

Nobody who uses special divine revelation as the fundamental category in theology and who is still prepared to talk of other initiatives from God to man, either through nature, that is, through natural, 'secular' existence in God's world, or through inner divine access to the spirit of man, can evade the kind of question which his Maynooth critics put to Lonergan. There is no point in trying to obfuscate this issue by talking about the regrettable Roman Catholic authoritarianism of some of Lonergan's thought. If a special divine revelation leaves a deposit of particular truth, then expression of that truth must sound as dogmatic on the lips of a twentieth-century Edinburgh professor as it would on the lips of any Roman Pope.

Pannenberg, for instance, if my memory serves me right with what he said at the Maynooth seminar, is one of those who lives with revelation as the fundamental category in his theology, despite the sophisticated refurbishing which that concept has undergone in his more recent writings. He says, quite rightly, that any historical event occurs can be researched (resurrected from the past), and interpreted only within a context of meaning; that the presumption is that this context itself belongs to wider and wider contexts of meaning, until this line of thought leads us at least to envisage a universe of meaning — which I take to mean an empirical world complete with source, plan and goal. But what can Pannenberg mean by saying that the totality of meaning appeared in anticipatory fashion in Jesus? And is it really consistent to add that the totality of meaning, the Christian universe of meaning, is yet debatable, being tested in history? An anticipatory fashion of appearance can mean either of two things: either that the total meaning appeared, and then the past can be made to yield it up; or that only part of the total meaning appeared, but the rest exists in the mind of Jesus and of God. Either way, since this is presumably God's meaning for the world, his system or plan or purpose, what we call history can only be conformity, not real creativity, and theology is the appropriation of the divine meaning from the Christ-event and from whatever other events in which it, or the rest of it, is thought to be revealed. What is the sense of saying that this meaning is debatable, tested in history?

The Logos divinity of the Christian West is back with us in another guise. This dominant divinity was chiefly characterized as mind containing the exemplar plan or meaning imperfectly revealed in this empirical world. Christians then talked of another plan, a plan of salvation, revealed in Jesus, the incarnate Logos. Asked to relate natural to supernatural, they said the latter was the perfection of the former. All the time they were dealing with a Logos divinity, a God of plan or plans which were revealed, and to which the empirical world in both space and time must naturally conform. The fact that this God has recently died in a cultural crisis characterized by new understanding of the randomness of evolution and the inconsequence of creative history has still not dissuaded most Christian theologians from using revelation (hallmark of this divinity) as the fundamental theological concept.

So God has two, or three, avenues of access to man, through creation, through special revelation and through direct inspiration. Theology is left in continual quandary. Does it appropriate God's truth from nature or history and then watch for the phenomenon of human conversion to this? (Perhaps it can conveniently rule out the revelation in nature by emphasizing the sinfulness of man, as if sinfulness could make a man selectively blind.) Or does it take as its datum that invitation which God is supposed to address to the inner spirit of man, and then wait to see what forms of profession and behaviour this will attach itself to or create? Not one of the critics of Lonergan has, to my knowledge, answered these questions clearly himself. Nor can any of them do so because they are themselves crypto-transcendentalists of the classical kind.

I hope to show, in a book on the problems of faith which nobody is awaiting with any great amount of expectation, that the only way to solve this problem is to remove revelation from its rôle as the fundamental category of theology; to make it instead a second and secondary category to the category of faith, which is the basic datum of theology. Not that the book was written to solve this problem. It arose, rather, out of reflection on the twin concepts of faith and revelation. Part of its thesis is this: at this present point of time my empirical, 'secular' world offers me access to acknowledgment of a ground of its being and mine. It contains the perennial prospect of faith. Add historical perspective to this native access of mine to religious faith and I begin to recognize the specific type of faith which my experience, shaped by my history, opens up to me. I recognize this as one recognizes past editions of one's present person, despite difference and by contrast with others. I know that it is great historical figures of faith that shape my religious experience, just as it is great historical figures in other areas of life that shape the rest of my human experience. Of this tradition I am at once the inheritor, the formed result and the evaluator. These factors make it the vehicle of my hope that I can adapt it so as to create a new, but continuous future.

Because such a figure, in my case Jesus, and such a tradition fashion my faith, I naturally speak of them as God's work. I say God was in them as if I caught him in the act, saw him, knew him directly, could look at things from his side. In short, I speak revelation language. The very conviction of my faith demands this. No harm is done provided that I neither get nor convey the impression that I know God's truth or plan or mind, in whole or in part, from God's side. I am the inheritor of Jesus' kind of faith and of his kind of life-style and I am blessed with the hope that, if I adapt these creatively to my present world, I am moving towards a future with God which he did not plan without me. My statements that God did this, or God wills that, my revelation talk, in short, says more about the conviction of my faith than it says about the mind of God. I know of no pre-set plan of God, or deposit of truths revealed by God, or universe of meaning already chosen by God. In taking up the structures of the past, which my faith regards as God's gift to me, I find full scope for my free creativity, which is the very stuff of history. I can change or at least develop anything, formulae, meaning, structures, symbols, as I change every cell in my body, know my genes to mutate, and still remain myself. Faith, not revelation, is the fundamental category for theology, and it allows full scope to human freedom and creativity in this radically historical existence.

This is not to say that there is no longer any room for the word 'transcendence'. As Camus said, there is, perhaps, a living transcendence of which art carries the promise. There is no truth or plan, to our knowledge, which transcends history; but creative beings in history, supported by trust in a ground of being, and by the hope which their commitment brings, can creatively transcend every condition which the structures of the past or the rigidity of the present imposes on them. Meaning, always, is at one and the same time present and in the making. Of three great spirits — Hegel, Kierkegaard, Blake — only the last placed art at the summit of human experience and achievement. It is time for a return to Blake, for art is the supreme indication of man's gift of creativity.

THE TRANSCENDENTAL METHOD

One of the disciple-critics at the Florida Congress, David Tracy, made the point that Lonergan still had to develop his method, that is, his critically established process for arriving at the truth, into the theological sphere; that the ordering and description of the functional specialties which make up the theological task was not and would not be sufficient. Tracy had no doubt that this could be done. (FT 215 ff.) It is significant also that Pannenberg was slightly annoyed at the volume of criticism met by Lonergan's *Method in Theology* at the Maynooth seminar, because he was convinced that, whatever the faults in Lonergan's attempt, he had tackled a job which could and must be done.

But it is impossible to have a critically established transcendental method unless there is transcendental truth after the classical manner. What Lonergan offers us in fact is a good deal of fairly good insight and advice in the course of describing many of his functional specialties. To say that his transcendental method, which is substantially contained in his transcendental precepts (Be attentive, Be intelligent, Be reasonable, Be responsible — to which he adds rather in congruously, in one of his more sermon-like passages, Be in love), is at the heart of the more specific methods and has a normative and critical function within them, is as naïve as it is to claim that a purely formal principle like 'Do good and avoid evil' could play a critical methodological rôle in the search for good and evil in concrete affairs of human life. His insistence that this transcendental method is basically beyond revision has all the brazen naïveté and lack of respect for concrete circumstances of Catch 22.

In one of the lighter moments of the Maynooth seminar, Professor Jaki from Princeton compared *Method in Theology* to the *Canterbury Tales*. One could learn a lot about humanity at that era from the *Canterbury Tales*, he said, but if one wished to get from London to Canterbury, the book would be useless. He said that to point the truth that the practising scientist allows his method to be dictated by his subject matter and is therefore reluctant to talk or teach method except in the process of working with his concrete problems as these exist at any particular time.

The scholar of today looks for patterns of regularity in the present and for patterns of consistency in the past, and he is seldom more than very partially successful. The technologist, the creative spirit of today, tries to retain the best of what has come down to him in his building of a new future, thus to keep continuity with the past. Again he is seldom more than very partially successful.

Man is a creative agent as well as being a knower, he makes a real difference in reality, and reality is really random as well as orderly. Man is evolving, too, in mind and body, and he has growing power over the future of that evolution also, to direct it as he wishes. Methods of discovery, therefore, always depend on the changing subject matter of this evolutionary-historical world, and they never transcend it. There are no transcendental methods for creativity — the very idea is close to contradictory.

Theology must learn to isolate its own basic datum, or that aspect of the general datum of basic human experience which is its own, religious faith. Already different methods of procedure will be suggested to its practitioners than those used by mathematicians or biologists or even psychologists and sociologists (the new ombudsmen of humanity); though, because it deals with such a deep and potentially comprehensive area of human experience, theology will need to keep in contact with other areas of human research even more than they need to keep in contact with each other — not for common method, but for moving insight. Theology must learn to recover the past or that part of the past which men of faith are convinced is God's special gift — not in order to read God's mind but in order to receive the spirit by which to build the future, in the hope of an absolute destiny which as yet exists neither in reality nor in mind. In short, theology must learn to live in the newly-discovered world of radical historicity and, as it does so, Lonergan's transcendental method will be as much use to it as the hearty advice: 'use your head and do the best you can with what you have.'

NOTE

1 Darton, Longman and Todd, London 1972; referred to hereafter as MT. Lonergan's *Insight: A Study of Human Understanding* (New York 1970) will be referred to as I; and P. MCSHANE (ed.), *Foundations of Theology*, Papers of the Florida Congress, 1970 (Dublin 1971) will be referred to as FT.

Some Questions on the Place of Believing Experience in the Work of Bernard Lonergan

Jean-Pierre Jossua, O.P.

GENERAL CONSIDERATIONS

Bernard Lonergan's work is almost unknown in France outside the enclaves of transcendental Thomism, which have been confronted with his vigorous earlier work *Insight*. *Insight* is not a specifically theological book. This enabled me to come fresh to his more recent essay in methodology, *Method in Theology*, and I took it up for the Maynooth Seminar with some anticipation, because I well know the reputation of the author in other parts of the world.

This book — which I need not outline and which I presume is familiar to the reader — is an impressive work. Whatever reservations one may express later, it must be taken seriously. It is the fruit of long reflection, and a work of originality very different from others which repeat in a dull manner what has been said elsewhere. It is closely reasoned, a work of great heart, attempting as it does at the present moment to offer a general method in theology and the religious sciences. Above all, we have here a work which has no intention of resting on, or returning to forms of interpretation which in the past made for the unity of a narrow, protected, clerical theology. On the contrary, Lonergan gives full scope to modern thinking, and his work aims at assuring theology of an honoured place in present-day scientific research. The book is also marked by a high degree of culture. Further, it has a greater sense of historical relativity than is common among systematic theologians.

Nevertheless, it is clear that Lonergan's work has left more dissatisfied theologians than grateful ones in its wake. This reaction predominated at the Maynooth seminar, and it may be predicted with some confidence that this trend will continue, at least in the near future. During the seminar much weight was rightly given to a point made by Karl Rahner[1] on the occasion of the partial publication of Lonergan's research: it is a fundamental mistake to construct a method *a priori*; this contradicts the elementary rules of epistemology, and does an injustice to the proper object of theology. I feel this objection would be very serious were it to apply fully, but this is not true in our case. The general methodological considerations which Lonergan elaborates in the first chapter, in the form of a universal theory of knowledge, have not the rigorous structural rôle in theological method which the author claims. Beneath the famous 'functional specialties' I detect a certain empiricism when he lists theological activities which are employed in practice. Only then does one arrive at a methodological classification, which is, perhaps, somewhat contrived.[2] The author could have met the objection by first presenting the method demanded by the nature of theology and then developing options which follow from the theory of knowledge set forth in *Insight*.

It is not my task here to treat of the real difficulties raised by the work as a whole. In passing I should like to mention three difficulties which indicate where one should seek the source of the dissatisfaction mentioned earlier.

The first is that each of the proper activities of theology listed by Lonergan is defined and described in a way that is peculiar to him, even if they do not lead to the principles that he sets out: they will, inevitably, be a bone of contention to anyone who engages in theological debate, and who conceives them differently. How can he hope to achieve agreement, for example, on his own particular concept of interpretation, or his concept of systematic theology? If there is no such agreement, what remains then of the 'method' except a mere list of operations, useful though this is?

The second difficulty is the ambiguity that arises between the constituent *moments*, which an analysis of activities discovers, and the *tasks* divided among various scholars. Lonergan attaches much importance to the division among team-mates of the operations discovered by analysis, as helping to solve the problem of collaboration between disciplines. The principles underlying the division are not clear. The division of labour that seems to be most clearly possible (i.e. specialties 1 and 3) is eventually deceptive.[3] Appropriating these results of theological activity is something else, and the allocation of the other 'specialties' is still more questionable. Is it not the case that the univocal model of 'scientific theology' which underlies this thinking is once again deceptive?

The third difficulty is clearly the most serious. It seems to me that the analysis of the act of knowing is less important structurally than might appear. But I think that the religious psychology and general anthropology of chapters 3 and 5 have considerable weight in the elaboration of the second part, and they raise many difficult philosophical problems. It is vain to hope that one can get theologians to agree on them, since in these matters they have a variety of philosophical options. It would be naïve to imagine that they will not be irritated with a claim to have achieved a unity of theological method on the basis of very particular philosophical positions, even if these positions have the reasonable exterior of 'common sense' characteristic of all thinking of neo-scholastic origin.

However that may be, a serious critical examination of these major problems is not easy. Lonergan's book is difficult — it refers back, explicitly and implicitly, to a whole *corpus*. Themes recur and complete one another. Many problems of interpretation arise at every step. What I have suggested up to now is in the nature of hypothesis; it is not a judgment on the basic issues. I should not like to venture such a judgment lest I reveal that I have not understood properly. I shall be content to mention a more precise point, and note some reactions. These reactions are not so much criticisms; criticisms may have been anticipated in a way that I did not recognize. Rather they are questions which, at least, witness to a difference of accent.

SOME POSITIVE REMARKS

One should say, first of all, that *Method in Theology* gives a considerable place to believing experience.[4] For me this is an eminently positive element. Indeed it has considerably more weight than the apparent hyper-rationality of the work. It offsets many hesitations I have concerning many of Lonergan's options. Before asking some critical questions — which are the essence of my contribution, as they should be of any contribution of this kind — I should like to point out the emphasis Lonergan allots to believing experience, and insist on the importance to me of this perspective.

1. It seems to me that the only useful way of reflecting on theology today, in an effort to map its course and to evaluate its prospects, is to begin with the concrete experience of the theologian in his thinking and his specific activities.[5] This is the proper starting point rather than a definition of the essense of theology based on the epistemological level of its discourse ('science') and its

object ('subalternation'). This is what Lonergan does (cf. p. xi) and for him it has the true sense of an experience, even though he links it more readily to the primacy of method which belongs to a culture of the empirical type. Evidently the 'transcendental' description and analysis of the different intellectual operations of the theologian is not the only way in which all this can be done. One could choose, in preference, to reflect critically and positively on the rôle that the theologian plays for the benefit of the ecclesial community or of society. This, however, is a matter of accent, because this perspective plays its part in Lonergan's method. This is particularly the case when he speaks of the rôle of interpretation, of 'dialectic' determination, the regulatory aspects of 'doctrines', or of communication.

2. Nevertheless, this mention of methodological choice is only an introduction. What one must underline principally is that Lonergan places much emphasis on the importance of religious experience at the centre of the theologian's activity. A certain quality of conversion — one is not quite sure if it is intellectual or spiritual, though it certainly is moral — plays a decisive rôle from the study of dialectic onwards (pp. 251-3, 259 ff.). No reader can miss the cardinal rôle assigned to an explicitly religious conversion as the basis of what he calls 'foundations' (pp. 130-1 and 267-70). Some have maintained that religious conscience is so structurally important for Lonergan that all the 'founded' categories derive from it by transcendental deduction. I do not think this interpretation is the correct one. It has the merit of attempting to overcome the strange hiatus which separates experience and the positivity of the categories, but it does this by a coherence that is not Lonergan's own. I shall return to the difficulty of articulating these two sides.

What is true is that the options which affect all the rest of theological work are made in the climate of conversion, and this approach follows right through to the end of theological work (see p. 305, to take just one example). Now it is common knowledge that since the end of the twelfth century Catholic theology has progressively lost the sense of this climate. On the one hand it has developed a rationality which has much value to the extent that it reflects a concern for rigorous thought, but on the other hand this rationality is so pervasive that it is destructive of theology, causes it to miss its object, and wind up with the senseless hypothesis of a non-believing theology, developing its syllogisms unfailingly. It is well known that the Christian East has been able to preserve this religious background of theology and that Protestantism has sometimes rediscovered it. Truth to tell, there is no conflict with the valid contribution of rigorous argument, unless one shuts oneself up in a narrowly rationalist conception of the life of the spirit. In any event, this primacy of believing experience, in the interpretation of scripture, as the beginning of all theology—I am conscious here of going beyond the formulation and perhaps the thought of Lonergan — seems to me absolutely fundamental. It alone can do justice to the authentic theological character of the Christian reflection of every believer and of every community however modest it may be. It alone can give full effect to the theological charism, which is far from coinciding with science or university professorships. Theology is not defined by its speculative or specialized functions, even though these reflect its differentiations.

3. No doubt one must follow Lonergan a little further and recognize a certain criteriological value (e.g. pp. 253 and 283) in this authentic Christian experience which is at the basis of interpretative activity and judgment. It is a question here neither of illuminism nor of infallibility. The same affinity with what is at issue — a spiritual and intelligent affinity which is also practical and effective — makes comprehension possible and should allow discernment. This at least should be so in confrontations within the community animated by the Spirit. I shall come back on this point, which, though not ignored by Lonergan, is not sufficiently underlined by him. It is not a question of inventing criteria, but rather of applying a rule of faith and life which can only be proportional in different cultural contexts.[6]

4. More generally, one may consider as fully justified the option which is decisive for all Lonergan's work, that is the option of beginning with the believing subject rather than with the intellectual objectivism of revelation or the social objectivism of Church doctrine. Clearly this is situated in the general tendency of Western philosophy for the last three hundred years, to the point that it is purely and simply 'modern'. But it also rejoins, as has often been emphasized, something essential in biblical personalism. Above all, it does not necessarily mean 'subjectivism'. The subject can and should be seen as social, historical, structured by culture and developing himself in culture.[7] Nor it is naïve in regard to various

critiques of the 'subject', which, without proving their point, raise many suspicions that existence and meaning have been devalued, and faith with them.

SOME CRITICAL QUESTIONS

1. One may ask if Christian conversion and experience, at least in the decisive rôle they play, do not appear too late in the methodology of Lonergan. I do not mean this in a chronological sense, for it is clear that he is not enumerating a temporal sequence, but a logical or fundamental order. It is here that there is the gap, which I suggested between the formulae I have used to express Lonergan's work (see 2 above) and his own thought. Christian experience is not only the condition of a correct understanding, but the starting point, the original fact — today, as for the first Christians who committed this experience to scripture under the impulse of the Spirit — and the permanent *locus* of theological meditation. Are not the data as Lonergan sees them in chapter 6 too archaeological and bookish? Should we not primarily apprehend in our experience the actual Christian community life with all its historical roots, and its re-interpretation of foundation events and texts? Another question, distinct in its approach, but which converges on the previous one: if I am not tempted to criticize the Kantian starting point of Lonergan, I wonder all the same if he is not enclosed in a Kantian perspective which is too narrow. Man is not only a transcendental subject but also an historical subject. Christian experience is essentially historical. Is it not because of his failure to admit this that the historical data remain outside 'conversion' and 'experience'? Is it not also this insufficient attention to the fundamentally historical dimension that involves a certain insensibility to the problems of language? This too accounts for a departmentalization of questions of interpretation and communication, which should be co-extensive with the whole theological effort: these questions come too late and too much in isolation. Here we meet for the first time, in the midst of a profound agreement on the primacy of experience, a divergence which, doubtless, is quite serious on the nature of this experience.

2. The distinction between faith as an act and religious belief is one which is not dispendable in any theology. But it requires careful handling. One can run into serious difficulties in making a

rigorous division between them, in forgetting the original unity of subject and object to which such an analysis should always refer as to its permanent source, and in insisting rather heavily on the priority of the former. Does Lonergan quite escape this difficulty in the way in which he deals with the disjunction between faith (defined as loving knowledge of God who offers himself freely to know and love)[8] and the judgment of fact and value which religion proposes (e.g. pp. 41 and 45, 118-9, 132)? Are not conversion, experience, and faith understood as somewhat general religious attitudes rather than as determined intrinsically, in their very structure of act and experience by their correlative: God present, given, delivered, as man, in a human life, that of Jesus of Nazareth? Does one not find here a certain indetermination of faith as an attitude, a certain exteriority of the determination of the confession of faith, a certain apparent arbitrariness of the rule of faith? The resultant impression is one of an uncoupling of the somewhat subjective 'religious' side, and the dogmatic and ecclesial side, which seems to derive from a certain positivism concerning revelation.[9] In consequence there is an apparent dispersion of the articles of faith: if the Christological element is not determinant at the start, in the initial experience of conversion, faith has not that centre which allows all the rest to have meaning, situation and perhaps relativity. In consequence, Christological faith only appears as one among a number of articles of faith, and secondary and relative doctrines run the risk of being over-valued. This, then, is a second divergence, on the content of experience which one can qualify as a first form of indetermination. There are others, as we shall see.

3. One may indeed ask whether the experience evoked in this book (or more widely the experience that is presupposed in the analyses developed there) is not also relatively undetermined in another way. Is experience not visualized too exclusively as an interior experience, a religious experience, if you will, though this term itself is very ambiguous. Is it truly Christian experience in its concrete complex reality, composed of different elements, full of tensions, expressed and structured by liturgical acts? Is not Christian experience historical, collective, communitarian? Granted none of this is totally absent, the accent is so placed on the individual and interior turning to God that the balance seems weighed down on this side. The communitarian ecclesial aspect in particular

seems very much in second place, and is seen somewhat as a reasonable and necessary consequence. Here we find the reason for a qualification already signalled when we spoke earlier in praise of Lonergan's insistence on the criteriological value of experience. This criterion is here taken in too narrow a sense, in too individual a sense; 'compatible with conversion' (i.e. personal) is not enough (pp. 247, 251, 283). Only the community is the depositary of true faith, and it is to its experience, to its communion that the search for criteria must be directed. I should add that in my opinion the criterion in chapter 10 of *Method in Theology* moralizes excessively. This is so not only because 'moral' conversion plays a rather surprising part, but especially because the fact of differences judged by dialectic is attributed too much to moral considerations. It is a dangerous enterprise to seek the root of divergences and the key to convergences in the presence or absence of the triple conversion. There remains a last indetermination: that is the indetermination of the situation of the individual Christian or the community in society. Before dealing with this I should like to pose another question suggested to me by the unifying rôle allotted to dialectic.

4. Whatever about the difficulties mentioned above, the religious psychology of Lonergan and his analysis of conversion belong to the best augustinian tradition. Following Maréchal they incorporate the resources that are peculiar to post-Kantian thought. They give a notable place to affectivity without falling thereby into agnosticism or anti-intellectualism. But one may ask if his conception of theology is not marked with a certain rationalism; I do not quite know whether one should call it scholastic or positivist. This rationalism does not easily accommodate the perspective I have just outlined, and only seems to accentuate the hiatus between the two sides. A very clear indication of this is to be found in the minimal position that is allowed to symbolic expression in theological elaboration. It is not a question of a theory of symbol (pp. 64 ff.) but the use of the resources of symbol in the expression, even in the reflex expression of the confession of faith, and in the articulation in words of the experience of believers. Another indication appears in the ideal of an easy and complete solution to dialectical questions, as if these did not normally reflect the inexhaustible paradox, which is of the nature of faith. Reflexion stumbles over this paradox, and quarries it endlessly, generation after generation:

one generation is never satisfied with the solution proposed by the previous one, either rejecting it or using it as a guide to further explanations. Perhaps Lonergan agrees with all this, and it may be that I am simply revealing my inability to follow avenues that his book offers in these directions. It is probable, on the other hand, that my last series of questions is more mischievous and that Lonergan's flank may be more exposed here.

5. Christian experience and conversion do not take place up in the air, but in places of human experience which always involve certain socio-political determinants. This marks the most intimate experience and still more its formulations and social correlations. In part, ecclesial structures, dogmas, theological doctrine are so affected. Here too is the ground where faith comes to fruition and realizes itself in a social practice, in the creation of a world. All this is evident, you will say. Perhaps: but does it receive its due weight here? Theological reflexion, the theologian's function, and even methodological discussions are involved here too; they have a social situation, they play a part in the confrontations of political life. Our author does not seem to suspect this, nor that the university status, which he sees as belonging naturally to the theologian, poses some serious problems concerning identity, money, caste, mentality, and power.

I will not insist on this but, changing the discussion a little, I should like to emphasize that to me it seems this calls into question the author's whole objective. This is not because he seems to ignore this dimension of things, but because he is a prisoner of university schemes that do not work any more. Indeed if he has one master viewpoint it is that theology should be considered as a scientific discipline on the model of other university disciplines. In typically Anglo-Saxon fashion he combines disciplines on the side of historical and literary humanism with those which belong to scientific humanism. Yet these human sciences, which are so constituent a feature of modernity, are not among the major preoccupations of the work. One may ask, then, if this exploration does not end in a blind alley, compromising the true creative liberty of theology, and the possibility of its being recognized by others. Is not the way of the future to keep more to experience, to live it, reflect on it, criticize it? Beyond all dualist and clerical schemes of 'dialogue' should we not follow an interior arc, which runs on one side from scientific disciplines in which man today recognizes himself and fashions his grasp of himself and his world, and on the other side runs from our cleaving to faith, and the experience of faith lived in the gospel tradition? Is it not in this way that a type of Christian experience is emerging, which will generate later a kind of theological language which has a chance of being considered by the more alert of our contemporaries? Our scientific friends, our political scientists, our psychoanalysts do not expect our theological discourse to offer a methodology similar to that of their disciplines. They will take us seriously as believers and theologians, if we give evidence of an experience which is lived and reflected on, in confrontation with their approach, and which remains itself beyond this confrontation.

CONCLUSION

I am afraid that this short analysis shows that notwithstanding Bernard Lonergan's attempt at clarification and synthesis, there remain quite a number of considerable problems that one encounters at every step. To these problems there are various solutions according to basic perspectives which are peculiar to each theologian or to different theological climates. Lonergan's classification of the tasks of the theologian remains a stimulating one. His return to the believer's experience is highly valuable and fruitful. It seems to me, however, that no methodology will solve the basic problems of the theological workshop today, and allow us to overcome doctrinal differences due to plurality of instruments, cultures, situations, and options.

NOTES

1 K. RAHNER, 'Some critical thoughts on "Functional Specialties in Theology"' in *Foundations of Theology* (Gill and Macmillan, Dublin 1971) 174 ff.
2 For example the special connection between comprehension and hermeneutics, and again between judgment and history (these could have been reversed). When the scheme of mental acts is applied, does it really correspond to the general division of the 'specialties'? In the same way the adequate distinction of specialties 6 and 7 (p. 132) is not really convincing. Nor is their relation with the cognitive activities, and it does not become more so pp. 295-353. Is there not a certain fever for combination, of which there are disquieting signs, e.g. pp. 140 and 172?

3 The example of the 'separability' of hermeneutics given on p. 153 n. 1 is due to an ambiguity between hermeneutic activity and the reflection *on* hermeneutics.
4 I prefer to use this inelegant term rather than speak of *religious* experience. I shall have to criticize later an ambiguity which arises from too indeterminate a notion of religious experience, which is not sufficiently grasped as a specifically *Christian* experience.
5 I have proposed this order of approach in an intervention at the *Concilium* Congress in Brussels in 1970. This has been published in *Concilium* No. 60bis, December 1970 (French Supplement) under the title 'De la thélogie au théologien'.
6 Here I may refer to 'Rule of Faith and Orthodoxy', *Concilium* Vol. 1 No. 6 (January 1970) 56-67. I have treated this more fully in 'Immutabilité, progrès ou structurations multiples des doctrines chrétiennes', *Rev. Sc. Phil. Théol.* 52 (1968) 173-200. A more recent and more synthetic account may be found in 'Signification des confessions de foi', *Istina* 17 (1972) 48-56.
7 While leaving W. Pannenberg to deal more fully with the question, one must ask if Lonergan does justice to these aspects.
8 This in itself is a very fine approach which avoids the rather blind deciphering of the Unconditioned that is characteristic of Tillich's religious experience.
9 This, however, is situated in its historical relativity. I do not find, as others do, that it bears the marks of a confessional theology and that it is marked by an authoritarian and hierarchical ecclesiology in particular.

'Conversion'

Donal J. Dorr

THE EVOLVING EMPSASIS ON CONVERSION

If we assume that conversion is a new idea in *Method in Theology* we find that like Banquo's ghost it dominates the scene without ever becoming clearly visible to the audience. But the discovery by Lonergan of the fact and the significance of conversion was not something that occurred between the writing of *Insight* and of *Method*. The articles on *Gratia Operans* give ample evidence of his interest in religious conversion over thirty years ago. The second of these articles (now chapter three of *Grace and Freedom*) present it in thomistic categories as a *gratia operans* which is a *habitus*. In the final article he refers to the distinction made by Aquinas between this kind of conversion and two other types — the perfect conversion of the beatific vision and the preparatory conversion which does not involve the infusion of a 'habit'.[1] The book *Insight* might be fairly accurately described as an account of, and an invitation to, intellectual conversion; and it contains as well important material on moral conversion — some of which (for instance the sections on bias) are referred to frequently when morality is being treated in *Method*. It is not surprising then that *Method* has no comprehensive and systemtic treatment of conversion. In the case of the notion of conversion, even more than other key notions in *Method*, Lonergan's treatment of the topic must be understood against the background of his earlier writings. Not, of course, that one can assume that he has simply adopted as his own his interpretation of the views of St. Thomas. One must keep in mind his fundamental approach which he has most clearly and most recently articulated as follows:

> The fact is that my aim is *vetera novis augere et perficere*. . . . Basically it is a matter of deriving basic terms and relations from the data of consciousness, of accepting traditional metaphysics in the sense that is isomorphic with these basic terms and relations and of rejecting traditional metaphysics in any sense that is not the to-be-known of human cognitional activity.[2]

In the light of this programme of action one can understand better why Lonergan is taken by the notion of conversion. For, unlike such metaphysical categories as 'entitative and operative habits', conversion suggests primarily a dynamic and *conscious* happening. So it can be a starting-point for one who derives his basic terms and relations from the data of consciousness. Lonergan's own account (*Method*, p. 107) of how the gift of God's love really is sanctifying grace but differs from it notionally, brings out this point very well and illustrates the difference between the *Gratia Operans* articles and *Method* (cf. also *Method*, pp. 288-9).

The word 'conversion' is seldom used in Lonergan's writings up to a few years ago. But we have said enough to indicate that the word refers to realities or occurrences that have been perhaps *the* major interest of Lonergan for more than a generation. In this brief article we cannot attempt to trace the development of his notion of conversion over that period; nor can we hope to analyse its full significance. Our aim here is a modest one which can be summed up briefly. We shall propose and defend two propositions:

1. Conversion is so important from a theological point of view that if it did not exist something like it would have to be invented.

2. There is no need to invent or concoct it as a *theologoumenon* because conversion is a reality.

We shall take these propositions in reverse order.

CONVERSION IS A REALITY

For Lonergan, conversion is not part of theology in the strict sense. It is prior to theology. It provides theology with its object or subject-matter. Lonergan prefers to use a less static phrase and say it provides theology with its *foundations*. In his 1967 paper on 'The New Context of Theology'[3] he elaborates on this. A most interesting aspect of his treatment is that while he stresses the intensely personal aspect of conversion he appears to have no fear that this will lead him into the individualistic and privatizing tendencies which have plagued those religious traditions that stress conversion. He points out that those who are converted can form a community and give rise to a historical tradition. In this way conversion is objectified and can be studied by theology, without becoming fossilized.

Theology studies not some lifeless object but living religion; and, for Lonergan, religious conversion in its fullest sense *is* religion. What he means by conversion is not everything that the sociologist and psychologist will cover under the heading 'religion' but those aspects which make religion 'come alive'. Conversion does not refer to a religion that is notional or nominal but to religion that is alive in the sense that it is believed in by mature human beings.

Religious conversion, in the sense just referred to, is a fact. It is at the heart of all the great religious traditions and is stressed particularly in Christianity. It is rather unfortunate that in recent centuries various factors have contributed to a certain playing down, in the Catholic tradition, of the experienced aspects of religion. But even this cannot disguise the importance of conversion in the lives of great and of ordinary Christians. The Protestant Churches have, of course, always stressed the importance of the conversion-experience of men such as Paul, Augustine, Luther and Wesley, even though they too have been rather 'scared off' by the dangers of extremism.

It makes sense then for Lonergan to take religious conversion as a 'first', an event which in a sense is self-authenticating (*Method* pp. 283-4). Whether or not he is right to use the *word* 'conversion' is another question. It might be argued that it is misleading and has a bad history: its long association with fundamentalism and revivalism make it somewhat less than 'respectable'. In these traditions far too much stress is laid on the value of a single climactic conversion-experience. The suddenness of the conversion is often taken as a sign of its divine source, as a proof that salvation is by grace alone. So psychologists like William James took a rather perverse satisfaction in showing that the sudden conversion was frequently the erruption into conscious life of something that had been 'brewing' under the surface for a long time. In response to objections to the word 'conversion' it may be argued that the word should be 'rescued'. It has a solid scriptural base in the term *metanoia* and for most of the history of the Church it did not have the misleading connotations which it acquired in the West in recent centuries. Furthermore, it may well be that one reason for its lack of 'respectability' is a certain rationalism which crept into theology and made us unduly suspicious of anything savouring of religious feelings. Perhaps a more serious objection to the term 'conversion' is that it stresses the psychological rather than the social and historical aspects of religion. Against this objection it may be urged that religion becomes 'living' only in the individual. Religious history and religious sociology have no ultimate significance unless there is a personal religious experience in which the individual appropriates his religious tradition or dissociates himself from it and seeks some other frame of reference for his life.

Religious conversion, as we noted already, is not confined to Christianity. In a lecture of 1969 on 'Faith and Beliefs' Lonergan proposes what he calls 'a universalist view of faith'. It amounts to something very similar to Tillich's notion of 'ultimate concern'. But Lonergan uses and develops a much more personalistic analogy — that of falling in love. In this and other recent lectures, as in *Method* itself, he argues that to be religiously converted is to be in love with God. The value of the analogy is that being in love is not an act but a state; not an unconscious but a conscious state; and not a passive one but a dynamic state which can be the principle of various activities. Furthermore, the analogy does point to a peculiar quality of a good deal of religious experience: the fact that it has high points of feeling and low points. A human love affair is quite a good analogy for a man's 'affair' with God since in both there is room for 'ups and downs', for spontaneous initiatives on one side or the other and for painful experiences of absence as well as joyful ones of presence.

It may be felt that Lonergan presses the analogy too far. Indeed at times he speaks as though it were not an analogy at all but a simple description of religious conversion. I don't think this analogy on its own is sufficient. It does not really bring out very well the '*mysterium tremendum et fascinans*' aspect of religious experience which Otto describes so well; Lonergan's remarks on this topic are interesting but too brief to be fully satisfactory (*Method* p. 106). It may also be questioned whether the analogy is not too Christian and too Western. It stresses not only the personality of the religious subject but also the personal character of God. This, of course, is quite justified — but the result is that the application to certain Eastern religions is rather strained. Indeed one might wonder how much the whole conception of 'falling in love' has been shaped in the cultures of the West by the troubadours and their successors.

TRIPLE CONVERSION

Lonergan repeatedly insists that conversion is threefold: in addition to the religious conversion on which we have so far concentrated there is moral conversion and intellectual conversion. Most theologians who have little interest in a theory of knowledge (and, astonishingly in this age of hermeneutics, there are still many of them around!) see little point in applying the 'religious' word 'conversion' to 'the elimination of blindspots with regard to human cognitional activity, its objectivity and the reality it knows' [4] and the adoption of a 'critical realist' stance. No doubt the use of the word in this way creates difficulties for those who would wish to keep a safe distance between religion and philosophy. But the very strangeness of the use of the term 'conversion' in this context prepares one to look for something unusual; and the break with commonsense 'naïve realism' is indeed experienced as strange and unusual. To accept that imaginability is no test for reality, that genuine objectivity is not spontaneous and that knowing is not like looking is indeed a conversion. And like religious conversion it opens up a totally transformed world for the 'convert'. It must be added that it is only within this 'new' world that the theologian can give any really satisfactory meaning to the word 'God' — so for this reason, if for no other, intellectual conversion cannot be irrelevant to theology.

A question that sometimes arises about Lonergan's account of a triple conversion is whether there is any real basis for making a distinction between religious and moral conversion.[5] There are certainly good grounds for wanting to avoid any sharp differentiation in practice between authentic religion and true morality. But I think Lonergan has good theoretical and practical grounds for distinguishing the two kinds of conversion. However awkward it may be for the theologian, it seems to be a fact that there are men and women who find themselves grasped by an ultimate concern, perhaps a transcendent hope or sense of forgiveness, even though they could hardly be said to be morally converted. And there are morally converted people who apparently find little need to articulate in any way an ultimate framework for their lives. At the level of theory, it seems to be an undue narrowing down of religious experience to interpret it entirely in moral terms. There are types of ultimate gratitude, joy, hope, worship and serenity which are deeper and wider than moral concern for others —

though they provide a foundation for moral concern.

Moral conversion, Lonergan holds, occurs at that 'existential moment' when the individual exercises 'vertical freedom' in choosing what he is to make of himself; it consists in choosing on the basis of value rather than satisfaction (*Method* p. 240). So much for the model. But the reality is seldom so clear and straightforward; for moral conversion, more than intellectual or religious conversion, usually seems to be very gradual. Even if there is a clearly-defined and memorable first existential choice in which the subject attains self-transcendence, this can be no more than the first tottering step in a slow and painful process. Indeed one might well wonder whether 'conversion' is the most apt term to describe what happens. To subject one's behaviour consistently to moral values takes time and patience. There are 'ups and downs' in the development, but they generally lack the unpredictable and dramatic intensity of religious experience. Nor is the process or event of moral conversion usually experienced as a 'gift' in the manner associated with explicit religious experience. Rather it is felt as a personal acquisition, something that one has 'worked for'. Nevertheless it can fairly be described as a conversion in so far as it does involve a decisive break with the past and the adoption, in principle, of a new life-style. Lonergan can find support in Kierkegaard both for his notion of moral conversion and for making a distinction between this and religious conversion.[6] But unlike Kierkegaard he does not set the latter in total opposition to the former.

FOURFOLD CONVERSION

A final question about conversion as a reality is whether it is threefold or fourfold. Is there a 'Christian conversion' over and above religious conversion and subsequent to it? It seems likely that Lonergan deliberately by-passed this question in *Method*, presumably on the ground that the precise difference between Christianity and other religions is one of those substantive theological positions which he can afford to leave open in a book about theological methodology in general. But one would dearly like to have the issue clarified since it bears on crucial issues — notably the very nature of Christian revelation. Despite certain remarks which give a basis for holding that for Lonergan Christian conversion is distinct from religious conversion, I think the main direction of his thinking is different. It would seem that for him *any* authentic religious conversion is in some sense a Christian conversion. The *explicit* acceptance of Christ in the second or personal phase of theology occurs at the theological level only when one moves from foundations to doctrines (though, of course, the basic options of Christianity have already been articulated and isolated in the first phase of theology, especially in dialectics). It appears that Rahner considers it a weakness in Lonergan's position that the uniqueness of Christianity is not present in it from the very beginning.[7] But, as far as I can see, the same general approach is adopted by Rahner himself in his various accounts of anonymous Christianity. It does not really deny the uniqueness of Christianity but seeks to find this in its unique ability to explicitate and articulate, and provide a historical basis for, the gift of grace and faith offered to *all* men. It is in this sense that Christian conversion is not a totally new and different phenomenon from religious conversion. What is popularly called a 'conversion' to the Christian faith may not necessarily be a religious conversion in the proper sense. It may be a significant change in 'doctrines', arising from a conviction of the need for a more adequate expression of, and basis for, one's religious experience. For one living in the Western world, religion should of course be mediated through the Christian tradition so that religious conversion and Christian conversion would be inseparable. But it may not work out like that because in our rather secularized world there is an increasing gap between personal religious experience and 'official' Christianity.

IF CONVERSION DID NOT EXIST, THEOLOGIANS WOULD HAVE TO INVENT IT

Having tried briefly to indicate that conversion is not a mere *theologoumenon* but a fundamental reality, we can now go on to the more interesting question of its signficance in the book *Method*. We have already said that interest in conversion is not the new thing in the book. What then is new? Fundamentally it is the *re-duplication* which provides the basis for a division of theology into two phases each containing four functional specialties. Various critics have expressed reservations about the need for eight specialties; some, for instance, wonder about the validity of a distinction between history and dialectics. But these are matters of detail in relation to the over-all pattern of the two phases. There can be little doubt about the light this general pattern throws on the relationship of the various branches or aspects of theology to each other. For Lonergan himself it obviously came as a great clarification: and it is much more intellectually satisfying than the pattern one finds, say, in his two books on the Trinity.

Conversion does not belong properly in either of the two phases of theology, since it is a religious event on which theology reflects rather than a theological operation. Nevertheless, conversion is absolutely fundamental to the re-duplication since the presupposition is that conversion precedes the second phase of theology. Grossly over-simplified, the basic outline is that in the first four functional specialties the ideally objective observer is 'listening' and discerning the fundamental options; in the triple conversion he takes a personal stance on key issues which lie behind the basic options; and in the four functional specialties of the second phase he articulates and communicates this personal stance.

If conversion is the basis for the re-duplication then obviously it is a matter of major importance not merely in the religious sphere but also in the theological sphere. What is this theological significance? Conversion provides the transition-point from the first phase to the second, and, more importantly, the link between the two. Lonergan has been accused of undue stress on interiority or subjectivity in some parts of *Method* and of excessive objectivism in others (e.g. his account of 'doctrines'). If he succeeds in linking subjectivity and objectivity it is chiefly through his conception of conversion.

The difficulty of combining the subjective with the objective is a major one for all modern theology so it may be well to situate Lonergan's approach by relating it to the modern theological 'scene'. The theology of the past fifty years has been dominated by two currents of thought which can be roughly designated as the existentialist and the reaction against it. By the existentialist approach we mean the trend which, with Bultmann, stresses above all else the present moment of decision. Accounts of saving events in past history and the anticipation of the future *eschaton* have their real significance in the existential meeting with Christ here and now. The supreme salvation-event occurs in the life of the individual believer.

CONVERSION: SUBJECTIVITY AND OBJECTIVITY

It is unnecessary to repeat at length the criticism which this approach is open to: that it evacuates history of real objective meaning and reduces past and future to the believer's present. Faith as decision has no firm links with any particular objective and historical content. The result is that the Christian faith can be progressively emptied of objective content by an escalating programme of demythologization; and it is difficult to know where this is to stop. In a very significant exchange of letters with Bultmann, Karl Jaspers argued that if Bultmann were consistent he would become a complete 'liberal' by eliminating *all* content from his faith;[8] and Bultmann had no good answer to the argument. Tillich, too, seems to have found it hard to locate any absolutes in the content of the Christian faith. It would seem then that an approach to Christian faith which starts from the existential subject has great difficulty in attaining objectivity, that is, in linking this personal faith to the public, objective, historical revelation of the Judeo-Christian tradition. Faith remains essentially a subjective and private affair.

In the past decade there has been a strong reaction against this 'privatization' of Christian faith. History has become a matter of major theological concern. But this history is not just a personal salvation history or a personal interpretation of history but real objective events which are seen to have revelatory significance. Pannenberg's account of revelation as history is perhaps the clearest example of the new approach because for him revelation in history is something very objective, which can be *known* rather than believed. Discerning the truth about Christ is a matter for objective historical investigation;[9] so in principle God's revelation is open to anybody with eyes to see. Here Pannenberg rejects Barthian conceptions of revelation and faith as set over against mere natural knowledge.

But this concern for the objective and publicly available character of revelation results in a very one-sided version of Christianity. This 'new Protestantism' is very 'Catholic' in so far as it shares many of the strengths and weaknesses of the anti-Protestant Catholicism of recent centuries. But despite its rationalistic tendencies, this Catholicism maintained an anti-Pelagian stance. Indeed it was this that led to a two-level approach — natural and supernatural — and that part of the 'Catholic' tradition is rejected by Pannenberg.

Whatever its faults, the two-tier approach at least brought out the fact that faith is a gift, an unmerited grace. This gift aspect of faith is so intrinsic to the scriptural account that it must not be played down.[10] But the 'new Protestantism', in vindicating the objective and historical character of revelation, runs into serious difficulties about how the human response of faith can be at the same time a gift of God.

Lonergan depends on his notion of conversion to enable him to steer between the Scylla of subjectivism and the Charybdis of excessive objectivism. Though conversion is not itself a theological operation it transforms the horizon of the theologian and in this way it has a profound effect on his 'doing' of theology. It offers the possibility of avoiding a completely relativistic pluralism even though one starts from the existing plurality of conscious subjects. There is a pluralism of complementarity which is enriching; and there is a pluralism of contradiction which is divisive. Lonergan is concerned to lay bare the ultimate sources of the pluralism of contradiction — sources which lie deeper than lack of information or failure to draw logical conclusions from premises. If, as Pannenberg claims, revelation is evident to all who have eyes to see it, how is it that many wise and intelligent scholars do not in fact see it? Lonergan claims that the ultimate sources of division are beyond logic and beyond generally available information. They lie deep in the heart and mind of men; they arise from differences of 'horizon' due to the fact that some are intellectually, morally and religiously converted while others lack some or all of these conversions, in whole or in part.

Lonergan holds that religious conversion is causally prior to the other conversions and leads on to them. This has an interesting implication: it means that the main practical hope of reconciling those who differ on philosophical issues is that they should all become religiously converted as a first stage towards the intellectual conversion which would resolve the differences! This may sound as though Lonergan were introducing a supernatural intervention to solve natural or rational problems. But one must recall the whole new theology of grace and the supernatural which avoids the problems of the exaggerated two-tier approach. Religious conversion is supernatural in one sense: it is the gift of God's love which is beyond the level of human achievement. But it is not supernatural in the sense of being uncheckable, unexperiencable and unknowable. Even more importantly, it is not limited to an arbitrarily chosen few. The gift is offered to *all* and in this very concrete sense it is 'natural' to man.

With this background, Lonergan can set about trying to reconcile his stress on subjectivity with historical and doctrinal objectivity. There is complete seriousness in his treatment of history. The aim is objectivity. In the 'listening' phase of theology the Christian believer can work side by side with any open-minded scholar in seeking the objective truth. There is no *a priori* limit to their co-operation, no point at which the Christian as a believer claims to have new information at his disposal. The Christian believes that other scholars should be able to come all the way with him; if, according to Lonergan, there is need for the triple conversion, this is not an arbitrary interference alien to the whole process but something that is called for by the human need to be authentic in search for truth, and the response to value.

In the second phase of theology there is also commitment to objectivity. His use of the word 'doctrines' and the examples he takes, as well as his analysis of the teaching of Vatican I, have at times given the impression that he has a naïve notion of what doctrinal objectivity means. It has been suggested, for instance, that he has a *simpliste* propositional approach to Christian revelation. Perhaps his very heuristic treatment of the topic lends itself to this impression. Perhaps, too, he has not yet thought through the whole question of revelation in terms of modern theology. But on the whole I am inclined to think that his position on these issues is much more sophisticated than might appear at first reading. For instance, his treatment of history and of the complexities of historical interpretation, his detailed account of different kinds of meaning, and, above all, his stress on mystery, show that objectivity for him is by no means the same thing as non-historical propositional orthodoxy.

But how is Lonergan's stress on historical and doctrinal objectivity harmonized with his starting-point in subjectivity? The key seems to be the fact that in his eight-fold scheme the foundations and doctrines which objectify conversion are the fifth and sixth specialties rather than the first and second. This means they come *after* the whole 'listening' phase and in particular after history and dialectics. So the theologian at this stage is not operating in a vacuum, in a non-temporal, non-historical out-of-this-world situation. Rather he is one who has studied the history of Christianity and of other traditions. His taking up of a personal stance is done *vis-a-vis* these traditions. He is personally appropriating the tradition in which he has found himself or else he is rejecting it on some key issue or issues. Because he is not an isolated subject but one situated in history there is room for a harmony of subjectivity and doctrinal objectivity.

Conversion is the attainment by the human subject of genuine self-transcendence in the intellectual, moral and religious spheres. But 'objectivity is simply the consequence of authentic subjectivity' (*Method* p. 265). That is the basis for our claim that if conversion did not exist, theologians would have to invent it. In fact we can go further and say that even when the would-be theologian is not converted he has to presume that he is. For what kind of theology would it be that did not claim to articulate truly and responsibly (however inadequately) the reality of religious experience?

NOTES

1 *Theological Studies* 3 (Dec. 1942) 558; *Grace and Freedom : Operative Grace in the Thought of St. Thomas Aquinas* (Darton, Longman and Todd: London 1971) 122.
2 'Bernard Lonergan Responds' in P. McShane (ed.), *Language, Truth and Meaning : Papers from the International Lonergan Conference 1970* (Gill and Macmillan: Dublin 1972) 312.
3 In Shook (ed.), *Theology of Renewal I* (Herder and Herder: New York 1968).
4 *Language, Truth and Meaning* 308.
5 E.g. C. Curran in P. McShane (ed.), *Foundations of Theology : Papers from the International Lonergan Conference 1970* (Gill and Macmillan: Dublin 1971) 55-9.
6 S. Kierkegaard, *Fear and Trembling* (ed. W. Lowrie) (Princeton University Press: Princeton, paperback ed. 1968).
7 K. Rahner in P. McShane (ed.), *Foundations of Theology* 194-5.
8 K. Jaspers and R. Bultmann, *Myth and Christianity : An Inquiry into the Possibility of Religion without Myth* (The Noonday Press: New York 1958).
9 W. Pannenberg, 'Dogmatic Theses on the Concept of Revelation' in W. Pannenberg (ed.), *Revelation as History* (Sheed and Ward: London 1969) 135-9. (Since revelation is *known* rather than *believed*, Pannenberg interprets faith as trust for the future — p. 138.)
10 Cf. G. O'Collins, *Foundations of Theology* (Loyola University Press: Chicago 1971) 90-1, 126-7.

Front-Line Theology —
a Marginal Comment on Newman and Lonergan

John Coulson

The publication of two more volumes of Newman's letters[1] at the same time as Bernard Lonergan's *Method in Theology* raises some interesting questions. I offer the following marginal reflections with some diffidence since, like Whitehead, Lonergan's books form an *oeuvre* which must be mastered systematically before any criticism at depth can be confidently attempted. But a comparison with Newman is worth making, even if it has to be from the margins, as I hope to show. One is immediately struck by a contrast in tone. This is Newman writing to Miss Emily Bowles in 1866:

> To write theology is like dancing on the tight-rope some hundred feet above the ground. It is hard to keep from falling, and the fall is great. Ladies can't be in the position to try. The questions are so subtle, the distinctions so fine, and critical jealous eyes so many. Such critics would be worth nothing, if they had not the power of writing to Rome, now that communication is made easy.

By contrast, Lonergan's tone is confidently objective. For him, theology is to be conceived 'as a set of related and recurrent operations cumulatively advancing towards an ideal goal'. The eight 'functional specialties in terms of which theology has ultimately to be done (research, interpretation, history, dialectic, foundations, doctrines, systematics and communications) are' intrinsically related to one another. They are successive parts of one and the same process. The earlier parts are incomplete without the later. The later presuppose the earlier and complement them. In brief, functional specialties are functionally interdependent.' (*Method*, pp. 125-6).

The systematic theology thus often thought to be the foundation of traditional Catholic theology is only a part of the eight-fold method; and in speaking of systematics, Lonergan makes certain reservations:

I am not proposing any novelty. I am proposing a return to the type of systematic theology illustrated by Aquinas' *Summa contra Gentiles* and *Summa Theologiae*. Both are systematic expressions of a wide-ranging understanding of the truths concerning God and man. Both are fully aware of the distinctions mentioned above. Neither countenances the separation that later was introduced. (*op. cit.*, pp. 339-40).

The reason why a purely systematic theology is no longer possible lies in the existence of the plural society, which has as many ways of life as there are meanings and values. The culture which has been superseded was static, normative and classicist. Christianity has, of course, never been simply identified with a particular culture; and pluralism obliges theologians to take serious account of the notion of development. Since dogma is 'a revelation of a mystery hidden in God', its truth 'can be revealed in one culture and preached in another' (*op cit.*, pp. 323, 325). Thus the Word of God can only be known as it is translated in the new context, and the task of theology becomes, in the words of Bishop Butler's illuminating paraphrase, 'to speak the word, once spoken in a context that has long disappeared, in ever new contexts and therefore in ever new "translations"'.

One is immediately reminded of a note made by Newman in a copy of his *Essay on Development*, which reads: 'Development equals translation into a new language.' Newman adds, Revelation is not of *words* — from the derivation of the term it is addressed to the sight.'[2]

But there are more specific references to Newman than this, and they occur in a central section of Lonergan's argument, when he is dealing with the necessary 'transition from the abstract logic of classicism to the concreteness of method.' (*op. cit.*, p. 338). Lonergan pre-supposes that our knowledge occurs in sequence or hierarchy. Beginning as preconceptual, it is transformed by understanding into concepts. But conceptual understanding is insufficient. The objectivity we seek can be gained only 'through the self-transcendence of the concrete existing subject, and the fundamental forms of self-transcendence are intellectual, moral and religious conversion'. The 'basic statement' of this essential movement from proof to conversion (whereby we make the objects of our knowledge subjectively our own?) is that made by Newman in the *Grammar of Assent*, when he distinguishes notional from real assent. Lonergan quotes with relish 'Logic makes but a sorry rhetoric with the multitude; first shoot round corners and you may not despair of converting by a syllogism.'

The contrast between Newman's language and Lonergan's leads to my first marginal query — whether what has to be said might not with advantage be said more simply and less technically, and why it is not so expressed. In referring to the dissociative effects of pluralism, for example, Lonergan argues that these can be overcome by our conceiving theology and the relationship between his functional specialties (and specialists) as a matter of team-work. Yet in describing the task of the eighth or 'major' specialty — communication — Lonergan rarely rises above what might be called the language of middle-management. Thus, 'the church is a structured process. As does human society, it trains personnel. It distinguishes rôles and assigns to them tasks. . . . Plans have to be drawn up for the optimal deployment of resources under the existing conditions for the attainment of ends . . . plans . . . have to be co-ordinated . . . and eminent and influential people . . . practical policy makers and planners . . . have to be persuaded.'
(*op. cit.*, pp. 363-7).

This may seem a quibble, but it arises from a deeper and darker question. Does Lonergan feel with sufficient force the irreversible and irreducible nature of pluralism, and of its relativising thrust? This continually forces the theologian from the comparative security of a deductive method to the slippery slopes of induction. In such circumstances, is it possible to speak 'of the distant goal of a comprehensive view-point' (p. 129), and of the 'logical ideal of fixed terms . . . and immutably formulated axioms'? (p. 138) Can such aims even be *conceivable* other than in a homogeneous, stable and therefore classical culture, which Dr. Lonergan holds to have been superseded?

As I have said, these are marginal queries which a proper mastery of Lonergan's *oeuvre* might soon answer; but I note that Karl Rahner also tends to take this darker view, when he argues that, in such circumstances, faith may have to be justified '*indirectly*', by methods which 'would legitimately circumvent the individual, systematic problems'. These would be directed to a 'concrete' intellectual and personal situation, 'and would not claim validity always and everywhere'. Rahner, too, cites Newman as the first to develop such a method of gaining 'a sufficient certainty' by means of a converging although incomplete proof by induction'.[3]

In this matter, Newman seems to me to stand with Rahner rather than with Lonergan — at least this is what the Letters show. They reveal how Newman's theological method is forged by the conflicts he experiences. He speaks like a soldier undergoing bombardment from unexpected quarters, as much from the shells of his own side falling short as from the 'enemy'. Thus he writes on Pius IX's *Syllabus of Errors* in January 1865: 'it is difficult to know *what he means* by his condemnation. The words "myth", "non interference", "progress", "liberalism", "new civilization" are undefined — If taken from a book, the book interprets them, but what interpretation is there of popular slang terms? . . . they are the newspaper cant of the day.' Newman's is a front-line theology; and the language is characteristically very different from Lonergan's or Rahner's: it is literary (and patristic?), where Lonergan's is scientific (and systematic?).[4] Thus Newman refers to his insights as 'ultimate points of vision', and of resisting 'those further conclusions which others draw from me. . . . I say as far as I can see . . . such sayings are not hints on my part of something I see beyond, but ultimate points of vision'. In 1866, when he thought of writing on the subject of Infallibility, he spoke of it as requiring 'the most delicate and cautious writing'.

In a remarkable essay written in 1945 and first published posthumously in the *Tablet* in August 1972, Christopher Dawson describes Newman's theological method as follows:

> It was only gradually that Newman became aware of the implications of his principles and the direction in which they were to lead him. His thought developed slowly and painfully. Every step was carefully thought out, as though it were an end in itself, and he often deliberately shut his eyes to the step that had to follow,
>
> "Keep Thou my feet: I do not ask to see
> The distant scene — one step enough for me."
>
> Nevertheless, his intellectual pilgrimage was a consistent development of a line of thought which conducted him slowly but undeviatingly to its predestined goal, and his intense meditation on the gradual unfolding of truth in his own mind provided him with a key to the interpretation of the mystery of faith in the history of mankind and the life of the Church.

What Dawson sees is that the source of Newman's strength as a theologian is that he allows the full weight and *pain* of the context to bear upon his general remarks. What the *Letters* show (and what Fr. Dessain's exceptionally thorough editing helps the reader to elucidate) is just how Newman's theological method and principles are situated in that context. In the years from 1864-6, for example, it consisted of arguments about whether he should found a mission in Oxford, whether he agrees that the University of Oxford 'is a Protestant substitute for an Ecclesiastical seminary', and whether he thinks that the principle ought to be admitted 'that the laity should be more highly educated than their clergy'. All this from his own side, while from the other in persons of Kingsley, Maurice, and lesser figures came the chorus that *Tract XC* was a disingenuous attempt to have it both ways — by remaining an Anglican while accepting the full Catholic doctrine. Why had he still not come clean? The climax was reached in the charges which caused him to write the *Apologia*; but it is precisely these never tedious details of a life lived day by day, which the Letters reveal, that lend conviction to the theology.

I have called this front-line theology because it is lived out in conditions very close to our own, and it is admirably suited for a time when theology can no longer 'queen' it over the sciences. But since theology, by definition, takes place at the centre of many disciplines, and has to bring such disciplines into a unifying focus, would the metaphor of 'teamwork' or 'team-management' not be now more appropriate? The difficulty in accepting this without some reservations seems to me to be raised by Lonergan himself in the powerfully argued section which I have quoted above (*op. cit.*, pp. 323 passim). It raises the question whether theology does not over-reach itself if it claims the same kind of disciplinary integrity as history, philosophy, law or literary criticism, since its subject matter — the Word — has to be found anew as it is preached or communicated within the pluriform contexts of a post-classical culture. Is the 'team' metaphor too circumscribed for such circumstances? Once again, a comparison with Newman's conception of the 'schola' — 'as a generalization for the decisions of theologians throughout the world' — may prove useful.

The 'schola' is the name 'for the Schools of the Church viewed as a whole', each of which has 'a distinct character of its own', and often contains 'to its great profit, able men of very different complexions of thought and of doctrine — as the old Universities did'. Without the 'schola', 'the dogma of the Church would be the raw flesh without skin — nay or a tree without leaves — for, as devotional feelings clothe the dogma on the one hand, so does the teaching of the Schola on the other'. Security lies in the very density and diversity of teaching, 'as forming a large body of doctrine which must be got through before an attack can be made on the dogma'. The 'serious evil' which now confronts us is our dependence upon the Roman school 'as nearly the only school in the Church', the other schools having been destroyed by the Revolution.

This is certainly a claim for plural theology, and it avoids having to be grounded upon an over-sharp distinction between classical and pluralist cultures (what is significant is just how much of the *non*-theological part of that 'superseded' culture continues to engage us). Can we safely go much further? As early as 1834 Newman speaks of 'our intellectual expression of theological truth' as 'providing, not a consistent, but a connected statement' (*Arians*, p. 146). In the following year, in discussing the threat of rationalism to a religion, he expands this remark:

> A Revelation is religious doctrine viewed on its illuminated side; a Mystery is the selfsame doctrine viewed on the side unilluminated. Thus Religious Truth is neither light nor darkness, but both together: ... Revelation ... is not a revealed *system*, but consists of a number of detached and incomplete truths belonging to a vast system unrevealed, of doctrines and injunctions mysteriously connected together. ... Considered as a mystery ... (it is) a doctrine *lying hid* in language.[5]

This leaves us with the question what kind of theological *cennections* are possible in a plural society? Can there be a unity of faith without a uniformity of belief? And, if so, what is the conception of language which makes this possible? To see where Newman, Lonergan and Rahner may differ is as important for the answer as to note their agreement — which is substantial. Each sees the need for theology to be done within the widest possible context, being compounded as it is of many disciplines, the abscence of any being destructive of the range and accuracy of the others. But the extent to which any discipline, such as exegesis for example, can claim to be prior to each of the others is surely the question which divided Christendom and keeps it divided. Whatever metaphors we may use (queen, manager or catalyst) to describe this function of bringing disciplines together, the question remains whether theology is not rightly open to the charges levelled at all inter-disciplinary activities — that it is not a second-order discipline, but third-order. The theologian has only one way to avoid this charge that, *qua* theologian, he will always be something of a jack of all trades, and only master of one to the extent that, *qua* scholar, he is a philosopher, historian or exegete: he must claim that theology has its own 'method', and then stick his neck out by showing what it is! Dr. Lonergan's achievement is to have outlined with great power and detail the terms and conditions on which he may do so today.

NOTES

1 *The Letters and Diaries of John Henry Newman*, vol. XXI, Jan. 1864-Jan. 1865, vol. XXII, July 1865-December 1866, Nelson, £6.75, £7.50 respectively.
2 Quoted in my *Newman and the Common Tradition* 61.
3 Rahner, *Theological Investigations* vol. 6 pp. 27, 30, as cited by Paul Surlis, *Rahner and Lonergan on Method in Theology*, ITQ., vol. XXXVIII, no. 3.
4 For example, Lonergan's description of the language of poetry is written from outside, and not from within an engaged response. Thus he speaks of poetic language as tending to 'float somewhere in between logic and symbol' (which poem has he in mind when he says this?), and as being found to be 'full of what are termed figures of speech'.
5 Newman, *On the Introduction of Rationalistic principles into Revealed Religion* (Tract 1835, ECH. i. 41-2).

www.ingramcontent.com/pod-product-compliance
Lightning Source LLC
Chambersburg PA
CBHW071230170426
43191CB00032B/1255